A Childhood in Depr

COME BACK
AND
SEE US

by C. Glenvil Whitacre
Edited by Carla Whitacre Mayer

Introduction

My father was born to West Virginia farmers at the start of The Great Depression. He was a sickly, lanky kid with an intense need to answer two questions about the physical world around him: How? and Why? Never fond of hunting or the rough and tumble world of boys during the Depression, he found his niche fixing things on the farm. Everything mechanical was a puzzle to be studied, deconstructed, reconfigured, or repaired. The family's old Fordson tractor was difficult to start with its hand crank, so the family acquired a 6-volt battery to get the tractor started. That battery opened a door to a world of Glen's inventions. He used the battery with the electromagnet from a Model-T horn to make headphones. He later used it to create a one-way telephone and a microphone. He often didn't have electricity, so he tried to use the battery to power an electric light. When that didn't work, he pulled a generator out of a dilapidated Model T to create his own noisy version of an electric lamp.

His father worked as a foreman on apple orchards, where he earned a dollar a day. The family was also provided with a house to live in, and a garden plot to grow their own food. My grandmother managed to feed a family of five by growing food, raising livestock, and trading for what she couldn't make herself. They moved from orchard to orchard, as needed, crisscrossing the Virginia - West Virginia border. Depending on where he lived, he was often without electricity and indoor plumbing. When I read my father's description of their spring house, I realized for the first time that his first refrigerator was a cold mountain stream.

It's clear to anyone who knew my father as an adult that he was intelligent and thoughtful, but looking back at his report cards and papers, he was often berated by teachers. His spelling was atrocious and reading was often challenging for him. We now suspect he had dyslexia before such conditions were commonly identified. Despite this, he ran a school newspaper, taught himself to type, learned to write computer code, and, in retirement, he wrote his memoirs. I admire my father for his ability to pursue what interested him, despite what everyone else - including authority figures - thought.

My father would go on to be one of the first in his family to graduate college, majoring in Physics at the University of Richmond. He would likely have been drafted during World War II but he failed his physical while simultaneously discovering why he could never keep up with his brother George at baseball - he was unable to fully rotate his forearm due to a break in early childhood.

He made up for missing the draft by working his entire career for the Federal Government. He helped create one of the early computer programs, known as D2PC, to aid the government in predicting the effects of chemical weapons accidents.[1] He was proud to help safely dispose of many of the Vietnam era chemical weapons. According to his colleagues, he was a gifted computer programmer in the days of card-fed computer programs. His work is still the basis for the government's modern day computer models for chemical accidents. But the stories of his adulthood are for a separate volume.

My father approached his memoir as a string of memories punctuated by detailed descriptions of machines and buildings. Depending on your reasons for reading this memoir, some detailed descriptions might seem tedious. I would encourage you to do three things. 1) Try to visualize the machines and imagine how they worked. Clearly, that is what he was doing when he wrote it. 2) If the machines have no interest to you, enjoy his childlike awe and thank God you are not using a gas-powered engine to run your washing machine. 3) See the Appendix for a Bingo game of

---

[1] Some of his technical research papers are declassified and available on the internet. For example, Whitacre, C.Glenvil, Griner, Joseph H, Myirski, Michael M., Stoop, Dale. 1987. "Personal Computer Program for Chemical Hazard Prediction (D2PC)" Link to research paper: http://www.dtic.mil/dtic/tr/fulltext/u2/a177622.pdf: accessed September 2018

"How did Glen Make it to Adulthood?" that lists the many ways he hurt himself - usually experimenting with some new creation. It could be a drinking game, but I'll leave that to your discretion.

My grandfather, Holmes Whitacre, died of cancer before I was born — likely brought on from the the mix of arsenic, copper sulfate and lime sprayed in orchards at the time. I am fortunate that I have some memories of my grandmother Lottie Whitacre. What I remember most is her face lighting up when we came to visit and her sing-song refrain when we left: "Come back and see us, now." Working on this project has brought new meaning to those words.

As I write this, my fifteen-year-old son is playing a flight simulator game on his computer with kids from all over the US and in England. My thirteen-year-old daughter is perusing social media as she sits next to her friend — both staring at their phones instead of at each other. What I hope this volume provides my children - and anyone else who reads it - is a sense of context and history. It wasn't that long ago our family kept milk cold in a mountain spring. Knowing how life was lived in other times and places helps us to think creatively about the life we want to live now.

My father died at home in December 2016. I don't think I ever adequately thanked him for taking the time to write the stories of his life. My own child-hood memories seem unremarkable until I am jarred by some modern day comparison — like the number or type of available TV shows or each generation's idea of what it means to have and be neighbors. Each of us grew up in a distinctive time, surrounded by unique people and circumstances. Take the time to write your stories. It allows others to "Come back and see us, now."

Carla Whitacre Mayer
August 2018

Textual notes

Despite spending most of my career in publishing, my father never trusted me to edit his work. We fought about it when he first gave me a manuscript to type, and I regret that I ignored his writing for some time afterwards. When he was close to the end of his life, he was anxious to publish his second memoir. Based on my previous experience as his editor, and with a tad more confidence in middle age, I decided on two objectives: correct spelling and shorten run-on sentences that I found confusing. He immediately noticed my changes in the final version and glanced at me askance for a long moment. Finally, he said, "Well, alright." I'd like to think we made our peace. I employed the same philosophy in this volume.

In the section where he discusses his parents and grandparents, he included no names or dates. I have included this information for clarity and added some details from contemporaneous newspaper articles, some of which I have included in the Appendix. My father was an avid photographer but never incorporated his photos within the text of his memoirs. I have added the photos and written all of the captions. Therefore, any mistakes regarding these additions are mine.

This volume was originally four different pieces

of writing covering childhood through college. Therefore there is some overlap between sections. I considered trying to intertwine the four sections together, but I could feel his displeasure from the Great Beyond. Therefore, I have left each section intact.

Any corrections or additions (photos or documents) will be welcomed by the editor.

Local historians and genealogists might find some of the following interesting:

- Detailed descriptions of local orchards in Frederick County, VA and Berkeley County, WV, including houses, barns, sheds, etc.
- Descriptions of local schools, including Woodbine, White Hall and Stonewall
- Descriptions of tenant farming (apple orchards) including descriptions of the work, machinery, and lifestyle of tenant farmers.
- Events/topics described that may be of particular interest to some

  Community apple butter canning

  Bee keeping

  Medical care before antibiotics

  Community butchering

  Early cameras and photography

  Living without electricity or indoor plumbing

  One-room schoolhouses

Early radios and radio shows

Depression-era wages

- Household equipment: kerosene iron, cream separator, washboards, early washing machines, Aladdin lamps, Fordson tractors, wood-burning cooking stove
- University of Richmond in the 1940's
- Family surnames mentioned :

(Primarily)Whitacre, DeHaven, Haines

(Also) Clark, Crumb, Flowers, Funk Guthrie, Harper, Hutton, Jameison, Jimps, Johnson (of Richmond), Joliffe, Kersey Luttrell, McNeal, Munoz Noya, Sheetz, Ussery, Woodfin

Carla Whitacre Mayer
August 2018

1614 Ashton Ct.
Wheaton, Il 60187
bookmayer@me.com
www.familymemoriesmatter.com

Table of Contents

The Whitacres

About 1942

**Lottie
Catherine**

Holmes Love

Velma Pauline

George Love

**Charles
Glenvil**

OldStuff: Some of Dad's Memories

After typing an earlier version of grade school memories for me, my daughter, Carla, suggested I should write more. Well, I did. So this is for Clarissa and Carla.

I am sure this goes well beyond what was intended and is more than anyone is interested in, but that is the way old people are. Perhaps, as the particulars of those "good old days" became more and more novel, this may be of some interest. Let it age.

Glen Whitacre

1995

Earliest Memories

My earliest memory is of a wood box in the kitchen. It was made of bare wood in shades of dark brown and black. It was about as tall as me. I would pull myself up on it so it must have been 1929. I was told much later I was born at home February 20, 1927 on the Luttrell Orchard near Glengary, West Virginia. There was an unusually deep snow and the doctor was met by my father with horses and rode in on horseback. Mine was a breach birth, which makes it all the more amazing that my older sister, Velma, was huddled with me near the stove by the time the doctor finally arrived. The house was a two-story frame with white clapboard siding. The most spectacular feature was a broad, open porch along two sides. The house was on a hillside so that the porch was one step down along one side but the ground receded to three or four feet at the back end. There was an American Wire Fence around the yard. The gate from the lane was pulled shut by a chain, weighted at the center. There was a log smokehouse in the yard with an overhang on the gable end.

Charles Glenvil Whitacre was born February 20, 1927

17

Glen with his dad's hunting

A dirt road ran along the valley dividing the neighboring property. A lane crossed a small stream, meandering past a willow tree and up to the house. The house had three rooms downstairs: a dining room -- used as a living room -- a kitchen, and a parlor. It probably had three rooms upstairs but I don't remember. Since my sister Velma had come of dating age while we lived there, we had purchased parlor furniture, including a sofa, two chairs and a Brussels rug. The furniture was covered with leatherette (a cloth backed plastic). I can't remember that room being heated and the furniture was always cold to the touch.

We had a spring house. I only remember seeing the inside one time, when Velma dragged me along on an errand. There was the open mouth of the spring at one end. The water flowed out through a prepared channel across the floor on the right side. The channel was just deep enough for gallon crocks to sit in the water. These crocks would hold milk for a day, cream for a week, or butter and cottage cheese for longer. This was the only cool place in the summer and was kept neat and clean.

Left: (seated) Holmes, George, Lottie with Glen on her lap. In back, Velma with her husband Ruble Haines.

The spring house was strictly off limits for me when I was alone. My mother's brother had drowned as a young man, and she was adamant that children were to be kept away from water – even the spring house. It didn't help that my older brother George had fallen into a similar spring when he was two. Velma was supposed to be watching him. She scooped him out of the water immediately and took him into the house. Desperate for George's clothes to dry before Mother returned to the house, she laid them out on the porch roof. The big downside to this plan was that as

19

soon as Mother was close enough to see the house, she couldn't help but notice her two-year-old son's clothes on the roof! That story was forever enshrined in family legend. Mother never learned to swim, and never got over her fear of water.

We had a large garden gate which was directly across the lane from the house. One summer while my mother was working in the garden, I collected some of the footlong green stems from onions that had gone to seed. These were hollow and I was fascinated with cutting them into segments using a butcher knife. I cut the first finger of my left hand deep enough to sever the ligament on the underside of the finger. As a result I have no control of the second joint of that finger.

Mother loved her plants. She had a fern which grew so large that she planted it in a wash tub when she brought it inside the house in the fall. Everyone who saw it was amazed.

I have an odd memory of the stretched spring on the screen door to the front porch. I ran my hand along the spring and watched everyone leave to go to the funeral of Velma's second child which was born dead. Someone stayed with me and Velma's son Eugene, who was two years younger than me. The somberness of the occasion was strange and confusing.

My brother George was seven years older than me and I have vague memories of dramatic interactions between him and my father. One incident may have been related to George cutting up my father's leather plow lines to make a harness for the dogs to pull his wagon. I remember this wagon because my brother constructed a downhill track for it. When he took me for a ride, I fell forward and broke off my front teeth! I have other faded memories of intense fights between George and my father. Perhaps I can't remember the details because they were too traumatic for me at the time.

Holmes with his dead grandchild. It was not uncommon at that time to photograph the dead, particularly if there were no photos of the person living.

I learned of one event that happened when we lived on Luttrell's Orchard, only after I had my Army physical as a young man. I found out I only had 40% rotation in my forearm. When I told my mother and Velma, they remembered that I had fallen off the porch when I was a toddler. For days after the fall, I cried when my arm was

The big trip to Dayton. Mae and Harry Whitacre, Holmes holding Glen's hand. Velma holding Eugene. Lottie and George.

moved.

I remember the spectacular fire when the neighbor's packing shed burned. It had been filled with pine apple barrels. The fire happened at night, I was out in the orchard with other neighbors watching the fire in the distance.

There was also an incident that caused me some grief. As I remember it, the neighbor girl, about my age, was running around in the yard, and she, as little girls of three are apt to do, grasped the hem of her skirt and raised it over her head. She wasn't wearing panties. I noticed, but so did my brother. He proceeded to tell it as a major incident of diplomacy, and claimed I said, "I show you mine and you show me yours". He told it over and over and my protests only made him enjoy the telling more.

Glenvil seated in the Model A Ford on the trip to Ohio

The big event for the family was the trip to Dayton, Ohio — an astronomical 500 miles away! I don't remember any of the details leading up to this, but I know now that Uncle Harry had deserted his wife and son and gone off on the train with a "mysterious woman". When he was heard from, he had a good job as an auto mechanic, had a nice home and was living with Mae, his new wife. Then with a great show of (relative) wealth he would come back once a year to visit his father and his brothers and sisters.

I don't know, but I imagine, on one of these trips, he talked up his promise land, "You just get on route 50 in Winchester and follow it right into Dayton." My father bought a new 1930 Model A Ford and we set out to visit Uncle Harry. I remember the car being crowded, but it wasn't until I saw some pictures from the trip that I realized there were seven of us crammed in a Model A: my father, mother, brother, sister, brother-in-law, nephew and me. To top it off, my sister was pregnant! Velma had married Ruble Haines and was now expecting her second child. We stopped by the roadside somewhere along the way, and I remember sitting on a pile of crushed stone eating a banana. My only other concrete memory was once we reached Uncle Harry's: Aunt Mae had an electric coffee percolator — quite a novelty at the time. Also, judging from the pictures, we visited an airfield and saw planes and gliders. Traveling from West Virginia to Ohio with seven people in a Model A ranked as an absolute adventure in my young life.

Luttrell Orchard was owned by a lawyer who practiced in Martinsburg. To him it was a mountain retreat. He would come to visit, and organizing fishing trips and overnight coon hunts and fox hunts with my father, brother, uncles and cousins. To help facilitate the logistics, Luttrell had a telephone installed — a real, honest to goodness, crank-'em-up partyline! The first month after the telephone was installed, my mother discovered she could call and order goods at the local country store. It was five miles from our house and was a typical country store and post office of the time. In addition to the phone, it had wooden benches around the counters and a potbelly stove in the center. The ease of making a phone call proved too great a temptation for my mother. At the end of the first month after the telephone was installed, the tab at the store was more than my father's salary! They learned, but it made for a good family story.

Above Winchester

We moved when I was four to where the family always called "above Winchester". It was a couple of miles south of the outer fringe of houses. The house was small, just two rooms downstairs and probably two upstairs. It was located on the edge of a spring marsh — a broad pond of clear, fast flowing water filled with green watercress. This was fed by a major Shenandoah Valley spring, where an underground stream, the size of a creek, breaks through the surface and flows along until it disappears underground again.

This water fascinated me. I think most of it was only about a foot deep, but I wasn't permitted to go near it alone. There was a wooden walkway set on posts across the stream to a neighbor's house on the other side. It was a large white house owned by an older couple. Their daughter's family lived with them and the son-in-law worked in town. This was also an orchard but I don't think they cared for the trees anymore.

On our side there was only a drive-through corncrib with a spray rig parked in it. There must have been a barn but I can't remember it.

There was a pasture beyond the fence, and halfway across the field was a deep ditch with two junked cars in it. These were open top, touring cars and hadn't been there very long. My brother crawled under the dash one day when I was with him and took out the speedometer and ammeter. They fascinated me! I still have the ammeter (somewhere) but through the years, I destroyed the speedometer trying to figure out how it worked.

The neighbor's house was interesting; it had a large parlor with a standing easel holding a picture in a frame. The living room was large too, and included a shelf with a big old radio on it. This radio was the kind with a separate exponential horn speaker and several large tuning knobs with small numbers around the edge. I don't think it had had batteries for a long time.

The younger couple had two children, a boy about my brother's age and a girl about my age. The father came to visit us once. My brother had played his son marbles "for keeps" and had taken all of his marbles. I don't remember how it was resolved.

One day when the girl and I were playing in her yard, she found a pile of little oblong dried white things under a bush. She wanted me to play with them. I knew what they were, that a dog had left them. I wouldn't play.

Mother thought I should take a nap each afternoon and she'd insist I go to bed. I hated this. Sometimes I'd just lie awake and sometimes I would sneak out of bed and stare out the window.

My brother went to school in town. He was reported for skipping school. He would walk downtown to the movies. He brought home chicken pox and measles. I got both. My grandmother came to help. Then my mother became ill with the measles and since she was an adult, everyone was very concerned. They covered the windows in her room for a long time. She recovered without aftereffects but it took a long time.

At Christmas, my parents made up a special treat for me. They stuffed a shirt and trousers and placed a Santa Claus mask and a hat on it. They positioned this in my rocking chair near the Christmas tree for me to find it. When I saw it, it scared me! I ran back upstairs. They dragged me back, kicking and screaming to show me it was only a paper mask. Then they repeated the story of my fear over and over to everyone.

In the early part of March we went to visit my sister on a Sunday. I had a bad toothache all day and tried to fall asleep with aspirin stuffed in my tooth. It snowed all day. In the late afternoon, when we would normally have gone home, the adults began to speculate that maybe the snow was too deep. I don't remember if we tried leaving together, or if my father tried alone, but we ended up staying overnight.

The next day the roads were completely blocked. My father set out to walk home. When he reached the main highway, he was able to get a ride the rest of the way. When he arrived at the house, the fire in the stove had died and everything in the house was frozen -- including all of my mother's house plants. He made his way back to my sister's house the next day, and later in the day they got the road cleared and we went home.

When the Apple Blossom Festival[2] was held in the spring, the relatives from West Virginia came to visit and stayed overnight. In that house, there just wasn't room for everyone. There were stories of the night, including how someone had slept on the ironing board and this story, too, was enshrined in family lore.

I think it was the neighbor across the stream that introduced us to the exotic grapefruit. I think we were told they were poisonous unless they were soaked in sugar over night. Two grapefruit would be bought on

[2]Image: Apple Blossom Festival, 1931;1406-thl, Bill Madigan Collection, Stewart Bell Jr. Archives Room, Handley Regional Library, Winchester, VA

Glen called the The Shenandoah Apple Blossom Festival "the Protestant Mardi Gras." Elaborate floats and celebrities participated in a huge parade. 1931.

Saturday and then, that night, would be cut in half and piled with sugar to cure overnight for that very special treat for Sunday breakfast.

This was the first time I remember going to the store for groceries. It was a small Ma and Pa operation in a corner house. There were several steps up to the porch in front of the store. We bought coffee in a rectangular cardboard box. The name on the box was *Caraja.* For some reason, that word fascinated me; I was four and a half. I found out many years later that the word is Spanish for "Hell".

Bunker Hill

At the end of that year we moved back to West Virginia to an orchard near the little community of Bunker Hill. The orchard was on a hill, as most orchards were, because these areas were too rocky to farm. The house overlooked the village and the stream, which had once powered the water wheel of a stone mill. There was a church, a high school, a general store/post office and maybe two dozen houses along highway US 11 and a smaller intersecting road.

The house stood in a large green area which must have been a pasture for cattle at one time. On one end of the clearing, was a big house encircled by large trees. At the other end, on the steeper part of the hill, was a rather bleak four-room, two-story tenant house. We were supposed to move into the bigger house, but the family who was moving out had run into problems with their moving day. So, we had to move into the tenant house first.

Before the other family left, they worked out an arrangement with my mother and father to have their older daughter stay with us for the remainder of the school year. She had become pregnant the year before. She had had the baby but now wanted to finish high school.

The big house had a large living room with an

open stairway that went up along one wall. The kitchen had a sink and a pitcher pump. There was a one-story L- shaped section, with one or two rooms that opened onto a small porch. Along the whole side of the house ran a long, screen-in porch. The two-story portion of the house had, I think, three rooms.

The long, open stairway presented a new challenge for play. I ran a long string from the railing at the top down to a chair in the living room. I had a pulley and weight from a sand mill and I made it into a cable car for ferrying various things down from the heights to the floor below.

The owners of the orchard, who ran a coal business in Martinsburg, had a telephone installed to communicate with my father. After the installation men left, there were pieces of coiled wire discarded beside the house. These fascinated me, but before I could touch them, my mother told me they were "live" wires and that I shouldn't touch them — they'd kill me. This was sufficient warning, but later in the summer I saw the wires in the junk pit at the bottom of the yard. I studied the wires from one side of the pit and then the other. I stared at them for a long time, wondering if they were now dead, but I still didn't venture to touch them.

It was while we lived here that my mother got her first, and then second, washing machine. These were the days of "a few dollars down and a few dollars a week." My parents didn't go for that, but it was also the time when appliance stores would deliver "on trial". She got a white tub Maytag delivered. The salesman showed her how to start the engine, load the wash and operate the wringer. She loved it. But the next week, when she tried it all by herself, she couldn't get the engine started. She demanded they take it back. Next they brought a square tub gray Maytag (for only a little bit more). She could get this engine started and she bought it.

My sister didn't have a washing machine for her family, so after that, she came once a week and they did their washing together. She would bring her son Eugene, who was about three, and we would play together on those wash days.

The water for the pump in the kitchen came from a cistern which collected the water from the house roof. The cistern was built above, or partly above, ground. As the weather became warm, the water began to taste bad. We grew accustomed to it — almost — but visitors didn't like it.

My grandmother came to stay with us for a few weeks. She was having one of her "sick spells". The doctors could never find anything specific. Some suspected it was an excuse for extended visits with relatives away from my grandfather. However, the "spells" went on for the remainder of her life and she died several years later of what was probably chronic appendicitis.

As part of the agreement to keep the girl finishing high school, my mother also helped take care of the baby on weekends when he came to visit. I think the grandmother kept him during the week. He was about a year old. Maybe it was the division of my mother's attention but I didn't like him very much. He had an angry-looking circumcision and he cried a lot.

The girl, his mother, and I were great buddies during this period. I followed her everywhere. I met her when she came home from school and followed her to her room and watched while she changed her clothes. I still remove sweaters the way she did by crossing my arms and grasping the bottom on opposite sides -- not grasping the back of the collar as most men do.

Now, for the first time, my brother seemed interested in school. I suspect it was the different school. He did homework. I remember a poster he made of a western scene. He cut out saguaro cactus from construction paper to complete the effect. It was a scene from a Zane Gray novel he was reporting on.

It was a very hot summer and the upstairs bedrooms were miserable at night. My father set up cots under the trees in the yard and we slept out there several nights. I don't remember the family ever doing that again.

One of the running irritations, due to my mother's fear of water, was the water tank at the high point of the orchard. It was a big, open topped, concrete tank, above ground, very much like a swimming pool. That is just how my brother saw it in the hot weather but my mother worried and harangued him to stay away. The only real threat was the temperature of the water. Fresh cold water was pumped in each day to replace the water used to spray the apple trees. My brother told tales of this pumping. It was not done by an engine but by the water itself with something called a ram. It wasn't until I knew some physics that I understood this, but it was a puzzle then, and very interesting.

Lottie, Velma and Glen up on the water tank @1930

One day I opened the gate for my father as he brought the spray rig in past the house. I then fell in behind and followed. A five gallon bucket that was used to mix the dry spray materials fell over on top of the rig and dry flakes hit me in the face. It was probably lime, arsenic, and copper sulfate. I had been drilled in how dangerous all of this was. I ran home certain I had been poisoned. Mother washed my face and made me drink milk to neutralize the poison. I hadn't actually ingested any but I was that scared.

The orchard had a packing shed. In the fall the apples were picked and then brought to the shed where they were graded and packed into barrels and labeled with a blue goose, which must have been the trade mark of the distributor. A great deal of machinery and a number of people were used in this operation. The fruit was carried along to a metal chain with specific sized holes in it. Apples that were smaller than these holes fell though and were collected in bulk for cider. The ones that passed over were then carried to a table of rollers where they rotated and the apples with defects were picked out by hand. They then went to another size chain to extract the intermedi-

Labels for orchard barrels have since become collector's items.

ate size and finally to a holding table where they were fed by hand into baskets or barrels. The apples were moved along on wide flat belts.

At the age of five, I didn't understand all of this machinery. To me, it was a jumble of cogs and chains and belts which my mother kept me away from, while she worked, by telling me it would tear my finger off. I played around in the big cardboard boxes that the shredded paper had come in. This paper was used to cushion the apples.

But one day, I got close enough to watch the designs on the belts move along. I followed the belt to the end where it disappeared into the table and around the return roller. My fingers were small and one jammed between the table and the belt. It only rubbed the skin raw before they got it stopped but it hurt. It scared me that it could have been much worse.

Apple Ridge

A year later we moved back to Virginia to an orchard called Apple Ridge. It was owned by an insurance broker named Jamison, and a men's clothing store proprietor named Sheetz. Jamison managed the orchard and Sheetz handled the finances which included writing the salary checks.

Although this was another state, it was only about five straight line miles away and was in the same kind of rocky, hilly terrain. The big house was very old. There was a right-of-way out from the front of the house along an adjacent property but this had been abandoned and had grown up with bushes. The lane in use came in from a gravel road on the opposite side of the property. The lane ran through the very rocky pasture fields and then through the orchard, rising to the high point, past the tenant house, on across the flattened top of the hill and then down the hill and to the left which was the back of the house.

We moved into the tenant house that first year. It was the usual two-story, four room, unpainted clapboard, but this one had an additional one-story kitchen and a porch on the west side. This house also had a cistern as a water supply. It was fully underground with a large concrete top and a chain lift pump. This is a loop of chain with rubber suckers spaced along it. One side of the chain moves up the pipe which is submerged in water, which lifts the column of water into a box at the top where it flows out the spout.

There was a shed with no door, for the car, and an attached chicken house. There was also a strange round concrete building with a pointed roof. This had been built as the base of a large water tank when the water was pumped up from the well near the big house. Now the tank had been moved to collect the water runoff from the big packing shed located out in the orchard.

Then there was the lime kiln. This was now a gaping pit in the side of the hill with a stone and brick arch forming a doorway into the lower level. The brick walls inside had been blackened and glazed from the heat. It had long since been abandoned for its intended purpose and was now piled full of automobile carcasses and other rusty machinery, all overgrown now with bushes and vines. Most of the machinery was too rusty to be of much interest and I was warned off by being told there were snakes inside.

In the eroded bank leading down to the kiln there was an outcropping of soft soap stone. There were layers ranging from almost white to dark brown. I found that these rocks would write on the concrete cistern top. I spent hours making designs, in different colors, with numbers and letters, all over the top. My father thought it looked bad but he didn't forbid me to do this. Rain would wash it off, or we could use a broom and a bucket of water to clean it. Someone, I guess it was my brother, carved me a pillow shaped piece from the stone with my initials on it. It was one of my private keepsakes for a long time.

My father's boss lived in the big house. He had

a boy a year older than me and a younger girl. The boy had invented a game he called "making springs". He would drive an iron rod into the edge of an eroded bank, back under the sod, and then dig down and find the end of the rod. He'd pour water into the hole and pull out the rod. The water would follow the cavity made by the rod and flow out of the bank. He had found a cast iron stove top with a small hole in it. He would place this over the hole and fill it with water and the "spring" would flow for some time. This was interesting, but once this was done several times the only challenge was to find a longer rod.

One day the boy invited me to go with his family somewhere. My mother said it was okay. They had an old but large car with a big back seat. We three kids sat in the back and the two adults up front. As we drove along US 11, he pulled into one of the beer joints that had sprung up when prohibition ended. There were angry words between the couple. He got out, slammed the door, and went into the tavern. Almost immediately she started blowing the horn. This was done by touching the wire hanging out of the center of the steering wheel to the metal of the steering column. When she changed the position of the wire, sparks would fly and the tone of the horn would change. As this process continued the kids became very quiet and just sat looking stone-faced. Eventually, he did come back and there were more angry words. I didn't go with them again.

Following a project which my Uncle Tull had worked out for himself, my father decided to build a wood saw rig from an old Model-T Ford. Old Model-T's could be bought for ten or fifteen dollars to make this conversion. The body was cut off and discarded leaving the dash, hood and radiator to cover the engine. The front wheels were left in place but the rear wheels were removed and the rear axle taken loose, rotated left to right and bolted up to the frame. The rear of the frame was supported by a kind of saw horse. The wheel hub was bolted to the frame on the left side and a special hub was turned on a lathe to hold a large circular saw blade in place of the wheel. The bolting of the left hub caused the differential to increase the speed of the saw on the right by a factor of two.

Tull and Mildred Whitacre

When the motor was started with the emergency brake released (also the clutch) the transmission would be in high gear, with the petals up, and the saw blade would rotate down on the back surface. A log was rested on the frame were it extended behind, and fed into the saw to cut it into fire wood. It was dangerous for the two sawers and very noisy but it worked. I saw how it was done but it took a few more years of experience before I understood the technical points.

This is not the exact saw rig but it looks similar to the one described.

My hands-on interest at the time was limited to the pop-up and snap-down little door, in front of the windshield, that covered the cap to the gas tank. One day, in the hot summer sun, my nephew and I found that if you placed your face down in the door's cavity, you could smell the gasoline, and if you did it long enough, you began to hear noises like crickets. It was fascinating -- and dangerous. We didn't tell anyone.

Then one day, on my own, I crawled under the

canvas cover of my father's Model-A Ford and removed the chrome gas cap in the same location. My
mother found me unconscious. How long I'd been
there and whether any permanent damage was done,
we didn't know. I didn't play that game again.

I started school while we lived in this house.
My father had taught me to recognize the letters of the
alphabet. These sessions were the only time I remember sitting on my father's lap.

Each day my mother dressed me and I met the
boss's kids as they came by. We walked together
across the broad length of the orchard and climbed
over the stone wall that marked the beginning of the
neighboring property. We continued across their field
to meet the neighbor children and then continued
down their long lane which came out on the road near
the little one-room school. The one-way distance was
about two miles. I don't remember this being a problem except when it rained, then Dad would sometimes
pick us up in the car.

The school was, I guess, typical of this era.
There was a small coat room with pegs for coats and a
shelf for lunch boxes. There was a table with a bucket
of water and a dipper. This water was carried in from
a nearby house by a couple of bigger boys each day.
The remainder of the building was one large class
room. All eight grades were taught there, each grade

was one or two rows of the interlocking desks across the room.

The teacher was a young woman who wore skirts and blouses that looked like men's shirts. The day started with allegiance to the flag, the Lord's Prayer, and a song sung from the Virginia song book. The teacher would then rotate her attention, first with an assignment to each class and then one subject with one class, leaving them with an assignment and then going on to the next. Listening to the other classes was interesting. There were all of those new words I hadn't heard at home and subjects like geography were fascinating.

At recess the only game I remember was prisoner's base. It involved running from one tree to another. I don't remember the point of the game except to run from tree to tree. I did overhear wild threats and boasts among the older boys of what they could do to the teacher but I don't remember any discipline problems.

I did well with my studies that first year. In fact, the teacher sent a note home with me one day, it said I could stay home the rest of the week; I was ahead of the other students in my class. At least, I think that's why she sent me home, today they call it suspension.

Even though we had left the state, my brother

Glen is on the left with his hand on his older sister's shoulder. Velma was 16 years older than Glen. Her son Eugene (right) was more like a brother.

continued to attend school at Bunker Hill, West Virginia. To do this, he had to walk a long way, in the other direction, across the fields to meet the bus.

He was fiddling around with his rifle in his bed room one day, the gun fired and the bullet went through two walls and over my bed.

The Big House

The next year we moved into the big house. The boss had been fired and my father had been given his job.

Moving day was usually the first of March, and as was the custom, my sister came and helped scrub and clean and debug. My father's job was setting up the stoves and getting the fires started. Every situation was different and took some considerable ingenuity, but a quick solution was essential. It was winter. Setting up the beds was the next priority before dark.

In the coming weeks judgments were made as to which rooms had to be re-papered. We had to buy and apply this paper so these decisions were not taken lightly. After the paper was bought, my sister, mother and sometimes an aunt would work all day papering a room. I began to learn how to help with this process. Holding the long strips of paper, wetted with the flour paste, to keep it aligned for the sweep across the ceiling was the most difficult. Then there was the trimming around the doors and windows; I learned this first.

Now that we were in the big house I could see all of this as home. As the lane went past the tenant house, it went through the second gate separating the pasture from the orchard. It continued over the flat part of the hill and then turned to the left to pass the chicken house, wood pile, smokehouse and on past the back of the house. Beyond was a large two story building half sunk into the hill with open equipment sheds on the south and an open drive through the shed under the east face.

Beyond that was an old falling down hog pen with a garage connected to one end. Then there was the double corn crib, the well and its water storage tank on a raised platform and finally the old log barn. The barn had been built from hand cut logs along the native rock ledge of the hill side. It was structurally sound but had few straight lines. It was like the crooked house from the nursery rhyme.

There was a small two room building in the cow pasture near the barnyard. It had probably been built as housing for temporary workers.

From the flat top of the hill a large green pasture swept down this gentle hill to the house and these buildings. The hill continued to recede to a garden and hay field and on to the straight line edge of an old woods, which was the line of the adjacent property. The woods were used as pasture for cows and horses. It had some open spaces but was mostly briar thickets of blackberry and raspberry vines.

This hill side, this green pasture was my summer domain. On the flat top was an old tree that a kid could climb and eat the sweet black heart cherries. From the top of the hill you could see past the house and the woods across the valley to the faint image of the Blue Ridge Mountains to the east. This hill is where I flew kites and model airplanes, where I set up my version of a *camera obscura* to sketch the house, where I tested windmills I had built to drive a generator, and where I tested the tiny kite I made to lift the hair sized wire from a Model-T coil to make a super antenna. This was where I made two separate attempts to dig an elaborate underground maze of rooms that never got any deeper than the initial two-foot hole, where I stood lookout for my brother, or where I laid on my back in the warm summer sun and dreamed in the white summer clouds.

The big house was very old. It was also log, but had been stuccoed over with square white walls. It was two stories -- maybe thirty by sixty feet. It had a large central hall with four open flights of stairs and three landings winding up to the attic. There were ten rooms, a large attic and a deep two-room basement. There was a two-story, screened-in porch. The house had a complete set of working wooden shutters with all the necessary hardware.

It had a one-story porch with pillars and steps down to the yard which had been leveled against the hill with a stone wall. This was the front and had once been elegant, facing east, overlooking the hay field and woods. It was now treated as the back and had fallen into disrepair. The paint was peeling on the porch and steps and the stone wall. The fence was overgrown with trees and brush. The grass had grown uncut for so long, that it was in clumps that I could never cut with a hand push mower.

In the spring, my mother's priority was to make the yard fence chicken proof. The houses we had lived in for the past three years had had no yard fence at all. My mother loved flowers and chickens would destroy any flower bed. There was a fence, but it had to be patched and the gates had to be repaired and rigged to close automatically.

In the house's much better days, a kitchen garden had been graded into a hill with a stone wall at the offset. It was below the old front yard, between the

Glen took this candid shot of his mother doing dishes. Life before they had indoor plumbing.

house and barn. The soil was black and rich and fertile. Unfortunately, over the many years, it had collected massive amounts of every kind of weed seed that would grow in this temperate zone, and by this time they were all perfectly adapted to this soil. As a result, as soon as you planted a newcomer vegetable, it was immediately overgrown by the native population. So, I spent many of the most unpleasant days of childhood crawling across that garden pulling weeds.

I realize, now that I've had my own little garden, that over those nine years we didn't improve the situation. As the various fruits and vegetables matured and were gathered, the weeds were allowed to regain their territory and, before frost, there was a full two foot stand of weeds topped with the healthy pregnant seed ready for the next year's battle.

The area below the garden now grew corn or hay. It had a well that was kept covered and not used. The other spring/well, two hundred yards above this well, supplied all of the water. The abandoned well had probably been dug for the slave quarters whose remains my father had taken apart the year before. The log structures were torn apart and used to build pig pens at both the big house and the tenant house.

There were two chores that remained mine throughout my childhood: bringing in the wood and carrying water from the well. All year long, the cooking was done on a wood stove. In the winter, we needed wood for the stove and wood to heat the house. Although the old house had four fire places, these were now considered too wasteful and had been closed off in favor of heating stoves. It was my job to fill the two large wood boxes each evening.

Mother and I worked together to carry water. It was a major task. There was no indoor plumbing, so we gathered water from a well about one hundred yards from the house. Daily, we needed water for chores and for drinking water, but on wash day, the job was herculean. Wash day took at least two washer tubs and one rinse tub. Wash tubs are thirty gallons so each would take twenty gallons or more of water per tub. That's sixty gallons or fifteen trips with two two gallon buckets!

Once the water was available, it had to be heated. Mother would boil some white laundry in a pot in the yard (actually outside the yard, but close by). This meant filling an iron pot with water, and building a fire. Once the water boiled, we dipped out the clothes and water and carried it to the washer. Then we needed to fill the pot again and start over.

After my mother got her new cook stove, it had a warming tank. We filled the tank earlier in the week and it would provide warm, not hot, water. On wash day, Mother would boil water on the stove to fill the washer but we could add the warm water from the warming tank to top it off. It was a relief, because it allowed us to avoid the arduous task of boiling the water in the pot in the yard.

Second Grade

For that second year, the local one room school had been closed. Now, there was a bus that picked us up about a mile and a half from home and took us to the school in the little village of White Hall. This was a four-room school. It was a cube of a building, two stories, with two class rooms at each level. Here too, the back was the used entrance; the front had a small porch with several steps. On the lower level the rooms were separated by a wide hallway, whose walls were folding doors. There were two stairways leading from the back entrance.

Upstairs was a storage room in the center, of the same size as the hall below. Each room had a wood stove. There was a woodshed in the back for the wood to start the fire each day and coal in the cellar to burn during the day. A well and pump were at the end of a walkway leading out from the back door.

Each teacher had two grades. I must have been in the second grade but that first year I had been told I was in the primer. Memories of that first/second grade room are confusing because this was the only room with a piano and the school assemblies were also held there during all my later years. In the second year the wall between the hall was folded back and the second grade class, with a separate teacher, was placed in this area. I remember being in this hall and hearing a teacher discuss the composition and color make up of *The Blue Boy*. Maybe it was something special and I was visiting.

White Hall School, picture taken during Glen's visit in the 1960's

I didn't do as well in the second grade class. Now there was vocabulary, multiplication, addition and subtraction — all of which were on flash cards. I just wasn't fast enough. I remember being secretly proud on a test when I figured out that 3x7 was the same as 7+7+7, but that kind of thing was too slow for flash cards.

Some time in the spring, my father's former boss came back to the orchard one day while my father was working and accused him of stealing his job.

There was an argument and some fisticuffs. I don't know any more than that. My father wasn't injured and the former boss went away.

At school the next day, the boss's son, the one we had played "making springs" with, accosted me on the playground. He called my father names. I hit him in the mouth with my fist. I was no hero, I then turned and ran back into the schoolhouse. We just avoided each other after that.

The next year, we were in the same classroom. Due to some odd coincidence, or maybe finagling by a teacher, I drew his name for the class Christmas present . Odder yet, he drew mine.

The advice from my mother was, "Don't get him anything, he won't get you anything."

My father intervened, "No, you get him a nice present."

I got him a pencil box. It cost a dollar and that was considered a good present. I don't remember what I got but it was a nice present, too.

The long walk to meet the school bus was done independently, though sometimes I met other kids along the way. I wasn't afraid to walk alone or be alone. I say this as background to an incident that happened later that spring. One evening when I came home from school, the door to the house was locked. I walked around to the other buildings first. There was no one anywhere. I went back and banged on the door. I can't explain the panic that came over me. It seemed there must be something very wrong. In the next half hour or so I had worked myself up into sobs.

When my mother and father came back in the truck, my only excuse for my action was that I couldn't get into the house. My mother said, "You know the key is up over the door."

This meant over the sill of the screen door to the porch. I didn't know that, it hadn't come up before. Now I knew.

Thinking of this now, I particularly regret this incident. My mother had decided, on the spur of the moment, to go with my father when he had needed to go to town on some errand for the orchard. I don't re-member her doing that again. I hope I didn't keep her from doing this. We did learn to leave notes and I was never afraid to be home alone again.

Family

My father Holmes was 33 when I was born and had learned many trades by then.[3] At some point he was a blacksmith, and still had a forge, anvil and other tools. There were many things he could make or repair. Heating the iron white hot and then pounding it into partial shape, then reheating it and pounding more until the shape was complete. I was permitted to turn the blower on the forge and sometimes to hold the cool

@ 1896. Holmes is seated in the dark jacket in the center with his parents, Josh and Sarah (DeHaven), and siblings. Sarah dies of typhoid/pneumonia ten years later.

[3] Fridley, Beth, comp., "Frederick County Virginia Birth Records, 1855-96" database, Provo UT, USA: Ancestry.com *Operations Inc.,*: accessed August 2018; entry for Holmes Whitacre, 25 June 1890.

George and Laura (Michael) DeHaven and family. I believe Lottie is standing on the left.

end of large pieces while he shaped the other end.

Holmes was the fifth of ten children. His siblings created a large extended family that surrounded my childhood. When my father began working at Jimps' Orchard, there was always the open invitation, "Now, you all come and see us." With no telephone, there would be no warning. All would be welcomed, and of course, fed during the afternoon. It wasn't at all unusual for my mother in the late evening when the last dishes were put away to speculate, "I think we had twenty-six today."

Holmes' parents were Caleb Joshua "Josh" Whitacre and Sarah Louise DeHaven. Josh had bought a farm when his six boys were young men. From stories I remember, Josh expected the boys to operate the farm while he traveled around the local country taking a male horse standing to stud. My father traveled with him sometimes.

In November 1905, Sarah contracted "grip[4]..and from that developed typhoid fever which later became pneumonia. Five physicians and the most careful nursing, however, could not save her life." She died in February 1906, which left Josh with six children under the age of 18.[5]

Around the same time, my mother Lottie lost her father George Washington DeHaven. He died in March 1905 at the age of 56 "after a prolonged illness of some peculiar form of stomach troubles."[6] My mother Lottie was only 11 years old.[7] Her mother Laura Michael DeHaven now had six children under the age of 18.

Laura's 17-year-old son, Hollie, became the breadwinner for the family after George died. In Au-

---

[4] Flu

[5] "Mrs. Whitacre Dies at DeHaven," *Winchester Evening Star,* Tuesday, 20 February, 1906

[6] "Mr. George DeHaven," Winchester Evening Star, 2 March 1905.

[7] Pine Grove United Methodist Church Cemetery. (DeHaven, Frederick County Virginia, USA) George DeHaven marker, photograph supplied by Dana Bostwick, October 2005.

gust of 1906, Hollie and a friend went to Harpers Ferry for a fire company picnic when, as *The Time Dispatch* reported:

> a cloudburst converted all streams west of the city into a whirlpool and into a torrent. They were warned to remain there overnight but young De-Haven's strong attachment to his mother, Mrs. Laura De-Haven, and her little children, induced him to make an effort to reach home.[8]

GREAT FLOODS IN THE VALLEY

Youth Drowned While Trying to Cross a Creek Near Winchester.

HEAVIER THAN AT JOHNSTOWN

Streams Beyond Their Banks and Great Damage is Done.

The Times Dispatch (Richmond, VA). August, 04, 1906 tells of Hollie's drowning

The young men attempted to take their horse and buggy across Back Creek late at night and could not see the extent of the flooding. The buggy overturned and both men were swept away. Hollie's friend made a narrow escape but Hollie drowned at the age of 19. Laura was said to

8 "Great Floods In the Valley" *The Times Dispatch (Richmond, VA),* 04 August 1906, page 5.

58

have collapsed when she heard the news.[9]

In 1907 Josh agreed to marry Laura with the condition that she find some other place for her children.[10] She found live-in servants jobs for my mother Lottie (who was only 12 years old), her sister, and her older brother. The youngest brother Luther was eight and he was sent to live with a family. He never changed his name and he never forgave either side of the family.

Shortly after Josh and Laura married, tragedy engulfed the family again. Josh's oldest son, Austin, and two younger sons, Holmes and Edward, were pulling stumps out of the ground using horses and a wagon. The *Evening Star* recounts:

> The older brother was driving, and the two younger ones were attaching the chains to the stumps. Little Edward Whitacre fastened the chain he had been holding to the stump, and called to his brother to "go ahead." The horses made a sudden and unexpected surge and caused on the rear wheels of the

[9] *Evening Star* August 3, 1906

[10] Ancestry.com. *Virginia, Select Marriages, 1785-1940* [database on-line]. Provo, UT, USA: Ancestry.com Operations, Inc, 2014, accessed September 2018, entry for C. Joshua Whitacre and Laura DeHaven, 05 March 1907.

wagon to rise about three feet from the ground.

Without thinking the little fellow ran to the wheel, caught the [wheel rim] to pull it back to the ground, when his feet slipped beneath the ponderous wheel just as the stump was torn loose from its stronghold.

The heavy wheel, with its extra force came down on the lad's chest and face, knocking out one tooth and breaking his callar bone [sic].

The two brothers of young Whitacre hurriedly took him from under the wheel in an unconscious condition, and after shaking and

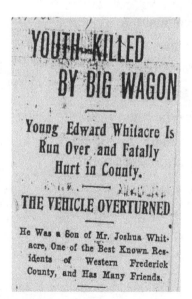

YOUTH KILLED BY BIG WAGON

Young Edward Whitacre Is Run Over and Fatally Hurt in County.

THE VEHICLE OVERTURNED

He Was a Son of Mr. Joshua Whitacre, One of the Best Known Residents of Western Frederick County, and Has Many Friends.

Evening Star June 15, 1907

60

rubbing him for some minutes he regained consciousness…

It was then about 6:30 o'clock in the evening, and the child seemed to brighten up and appeared to be getting along nicely, continuing so until about 10 o'clock last night, when he asked his brother, Holmes Whitacre, to come and lie in bed with him, re-marking at the time that he was about to die. The little patient ex-pired in a few minutes — just seven hours from the time he was in-jured by the wagon overturning.[11]

Edward was only 11 years old.

As time passed, my parents, Holmes and Lottie met at family get-togethers and then began to see each other socially. They decided to get married July 26, 1909. [12] Holmes was 19 and Lottie was 15; though both said they were 21 on their Marriage

---

[11] Glen's original memoir said Edward was fourteen but according to records, he was eleven when he died.

[12] Yes, you read that right. Holmes and Lottie were step siblings by mar-riage. It makes family trees really confusing!

Holmes as a young man

Application[13]. My father bought a farm adjacent to Josh's. Holmes and Lee (the youngest son) continued to run their father's farm until after my older siblings Velma and George were born.

After my father became a tenant farmer, his brother, Lee, married and continued to live at home and operate the farm. Now, in these later times, this home was what was known as "Pap's" to the eight remaining children, all of which now had their own families. It was not uncommon for two, three or at times nearly all of these families to visit Pap's on any summer Sunday.

I say "nearly" because Harry was the exception. He had gone off to Ohio, married and only visited once a year. This visit was for a week and this was a special week with parties staged at each brother's or sister's house.

Josh's oldest daughter, Matilda, married a cousin. Half of their ten children were deaf. Her husband was a farmer and their oldest son remained a

---

[13] Maryland. Washington County. Marriage License Records.. Maryland State Archives, Annapolis.

**Lottie as a young woman with Holmes's sister
Matilda**

farmer all of his life.

The middle girl, Nita, married a carpenter. In the 20's, they bought property in town, in Martinsburg, and he built a nice house over several years. It had a furnace, a bath, a gas stove, a refrigerator, a washing machine, a vacuum cleaner, and an electric toaster. But in the 30's, she had to fill the house with boarders to pay the bills. Her husband didn't always have work. Aunt Nita's was always the base of operation "in town" for visits to the dentist, the doctor or the hospital. Any and all were welcomed, fed, and helped with the technical aspects of their mission.

Josh and Laura had one child together named Carrie. She married a farmer who later moved to Martinsburg where he worked for the cement plant.

Austin was a farmer all his life and for a couple of years ran the farm, on which the woods near the big house of Apple Ridge was a part.

A picture taken at one of their Sunday gatherings. Austin, Matilda, Lee, Nita, Tull and Harry Whitacre

Tull's first wife died of cancer when they were quite young; he remarried and built a house in the outskirts of Martinsburg. He worked with inventions all of his life, went bankrupt once, and served as Superintendent of Highways for Berkeley County for several years. He had the first typewriter I was ever permitted to use.

I mention all of these relatives because once we were established at Jimps' Orchard, Sunday was fami-

Descendants of Caleb Joshua Whitacre

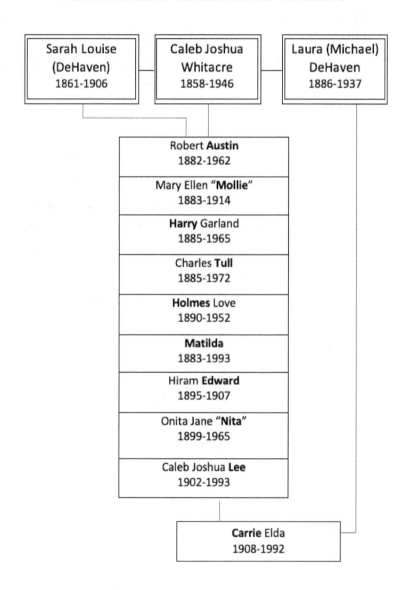

Sarah Louise (DeHaven) 1861-1906

Caleb Joshua Whitacre 1858-1946

Laura (Michael) DeHaven 1886-1937

Robert **Austin** 1882-1962

Mary Ellen "**Mollie**" 1883-1914

Harry Garland 1885-1965

Charles **Tull** 1885-1972

Holmes Love 1890-1952

Matilda 1883-1993

Hiram **Edward** 1895-1907

Onita Jane "**Nita**" 1899-1965

Caleb Joshua **Lee** 1902-1993

Carrie Elda 1908-1992

ly day. Relatives were welcomed unannounced.[14]

The men would congregate on a porch or on chairs under a tree and tell stories of hunts, dogs and guns. The women talked, took flower slips, showed off a latest dress just made, and, of course, cooked and served dinner. The kids wandered around in groups exploring all the new terrain of yards, pastures and barns.

The teenagers often formed a special group with their own interests. I remember joining one of these, as a much younger member, and picking a bullet out of my hair. They were firing a .22 rifle at a target set up on a fence post. The target was the curved steel wheel of a kids wagon (Radio Flyer-type). I was the forward, to report on hits. A bullet ricocheted off and hit me in the head. The bullet was badly deformed and very hot; it just left a blister.

Another tradition that was enjoyed was the house guest. Every year, or so, Aunt Annie would write that she would like to come and visit.[15] Her husband had died and she lived alone in Ohio. I guess she would come by train to Martinsburg, where Aunt Nita would pick her up. She would then trade around

---

[14] Editor added family names and dates to Glen's account for clarity.

[15] Annie seems to have been a nickname for one of Lottie's sisters .George DeHaven's obituary mentions a daughter Anna, but we have no record of a daughter named Anna, so I can only guess it is a nickname.

Glen's grandfather Caleb Joshua Whitacre, known as Josh.

among the relatives for one, two or three weeks each.

Of course, she helped with what ever work the women of the family were doing at the time and generally got along with everyone. She always brought her own shredded wheat. We never bought any, we didn't like it. She would heat a biscuit of the shreds in the oven each morning and then add milk and sugar.

Aunt Annie and I once had a long argument as to whether power lines and telephone lines were ever hung on the same poles. I was only basing my argument on what I had seen. Privately, I admitted to myself, she was from a different place and might be right there, but I didn't admit that.

My grandfather would sometimes visit for a week. He liked my mother's mush,[16] and would tell her so. It was the only time she would cook it. It had to be cooked and eaten with heated, sweetened milk with just the right timing, this was very critical. It was very good.

---

[16] Mush is cornmeal porridge.

There was another occasional visitor. He was an old hunting buddy of my father's. He would just stay over night. He teased me by calling me "Gimbel". I would object, then he'd take out his penknife, open the blade, and say he was going to cut off my ears. I guess I knew he wouldn't, but I didn't like this.

In spite of all this coming and going of family kids — maybe it was too many — I never knew any one long enough to become close friends. I was closest to my nephew, Eugene. We played together when my sister came to visit and sometimes he'd stay with us and sometimes I, with them. Eugene was two years younger, but he came up with an interesting construction technique. We all had wood piles with assorted logs cut into firewood lengths. He found you could stack these up end to end with a piece of board across at the second and fourth level and then drape burlap bags over this to form a wall. Place three of these against the side of a building and you had a play house. A tree house would have been better, but we could actually build this with what was readily available. When I had finished my own version against the chicken house, I added a wooden floor. Then from bits and pieces of faucets from old spray guns, some discarded spray hose and an old Model-T gas tank, I had running water. I dug a trench to bury the hose across the path and hung the gas tank on the fence to get enough elevation.

The tank had been discarded after my brother had made a pump-up garden sprayer. It had blown up while I was looking at it as the first bubbles began to leak in the top seam. Although I was blinded at the time, it was only for a few seconds.

I had found the cast iron stove top that we had used to "make springs" the year before, and this became my sink. Mud pies were no fun so there was no use for all of this, but it was great to see the water run.

My own amusements beyond carrying water and wood and pulling weeds in the garden included climbing trees and making a one-rope swing with an old tire. I could change this to a cross bar so I could do somersaults or "skin the cat" as we called it. I could hang from my knees, although once I tried to hang from one knee and fell flat on the top of my head. You can learn engineering by trial and error.

The well was the center of continuous activity all during the spray season, which lasted all summer. There was the chug and coast of the old one-cylinder engine with its two big flywheels, and the pulley driving the belt that drove the pump jack which lifted the water into the tank to refill the sprayer. I would climb up the fence to the platform and then pull myself up by the top rim of the tank to see how full it was, watching the gush of water with each stroke of the pump jack.

It was understood that I would keep an eye on the tank and pull out the knife switch to stop the engine if it was about to overflow. This had to be timed just right. The handle of the switch had broken off, shocking you if you touched it just as the coil fired. My father would get very upset if the water ran over onto the belt and engine.

Even when the engine was stopped there was the continuous drone of the honey bees coming and going to get water. The orchard maintained a colony of bees to help pollinate the apple blooms in the spring. After this job was done, the hives were moved into rows in an area about fifty yards from the house. This area was guarded by soldier bees that would come straight out of the hive and sting you. You didn't dare get too close. I was even stung once just walking by in the road.

However, at the well they were not aggressive and would not sting you as long as you didn't touch them, or worse, step on one. This, too, had happened to me. They would collect around any puddle of water left on the well top and water was usually spilled when I filled buckets to carry to the house. This was a definite hazard to bare feet.

Their stable watering hole, though, was the water trough. This was a long concrete tank set in the fence line between the barnyard and the pasture. The bees would land on the top rim or on the inside wall and crawl down to the water's edge. In the melee of coming and going, one would occasionally fall into the water. They could swim for a while but their sense of direction seemed confused in the water and many would drown. There were always some dead bees floating on the surface of the water. One of my pastimes was to hold a stick for a swimming bee to climb onto and then place it by the side so it could climb off.

Then of course, there were the lazy, dreamy days that seemed very long then, wandering along a path in the woods, or better, lying in the sunlight half submerged in the soft cool grass of my hillside above the house, sheds and barn. I'd stare at the white summer clouds that slowly tumbled, lifted and formed into imagined things that changed and dissolved away. I'd hear the muted sounds of a summer's day: the faint chirp of birds off somewhere and the distant happy chatter of the chickens as they seemed to gossip, scratching and pecking in their free-range search in the chips of the woodpile, around the buildings and out into the orchard.

You can't, now, recapture this era. There was no television, and, for most of us, no radio or movies. These get-togethers were our only diversion, our only entertainment, our only social interaction. Whether it was my age, the times, or the place, this is still remembered as the best of the golden days.

The Orchard

My mother Lottie had always raised her own chickens, turkeys and guineas, acting only as landlord or maybe nanny. The animals would, by instinct, collect eggs, set on them until they hatched and then raise the young. As landlord, this process was managed by picking fresh eggs, an attentive hen and providing the needed isolation, protection and food until the eggs hatched. She'd supply water, feed and a coop to let the mother do her thing. Occasionally, my mother had to round them up before a thunderstorm. That was all that was needed.

But now they were teaching agriculture in the high school and that wasn't the modern way to do things. At least, that was the message my brother was teaching. I don't know if it was his project alone, or a family project, but we bought a mechanical brooder. It was fired

Lottie DeHaven Whitacre and Carrie Whitacre Holliday

72

with kerosene and the temperature was controlled by a thermostat. Now, in the two-room shack in the pasture near the barn, the brooder was set up in an area enclosed with a cardboard fence and fresh newspaper on the floor to welcome some 200 store-bought chicks. These were watered and fed and cleaned after for several months and then sold as fryers.

As was the custom, with some knowledge of your family's reliability, a feed store would grant you credit for the feed over these months. However, there was no guarantee the selling price of the fryers would exceed the feed bill. And, of course, the feed store expected to be paid regardless. In our case, there was some money left over but considering the many, many hours of late night care and cleaning work, it was very low pay indeed. I think we used this brooder for a couple of years.

On the orchard proper, three men were employed full time throughout the summer. Starting with the first opening of the buds, the trees were sprayed with one course after another. The spray rig was a 350-gallon wooden tank on a steel frame supported by two large steel wheels. The front carriage pivoted under the frame of the motor and pump. This was pulled by an old Fordson tractor with steel wheels, also. Thus, it took a driver and two men to operate the two spray guns, one from the top of the spray rig to spray the tops of the trees, and one walking behind to spray between and the lower parts of the trees.

All of the time between sprays was taken up with thinning the now formed, tiny apples to assure that what remained would fully develop or cutting the grass and weeds that would grow between the trees. The open space between the trees could be cut with the mule-drawn mower but the spaces under the trees and the rock breaks had to be cut by hand. A long handled, three-foot scythe was used for this purpose.

It was hard physical work but my brother took the job as a form of training. It would develop muscles and he prided himself on this. To complete the picture he refused to wear a shirt and wore shorts when ever possible. He tanned golden brown and told everyone he was part Indian. My father didn't like this, but he did agree on one point, "He looks like a damn Indian." My brother persisted. This made it easier for me to spend the summer without a shirt, too.

George was the athlete of the family.

The orchard had been planted with several varieties of apples and some peaches. Each section of early apples was small and could be picked by the regular workers and their families in a few days. The bulk of the crop, the fall apples, was another matter.

In September and October the work force increased to twenty or thirty. These seasonal workers came from our families and from the families of small farms in the surrounding area that welcomed the extra work for their year's cash income.

Approximately ten people worked in the packing shed. Two workers manned the farm truck to deliver the empty boxes to the orchard and the full boxes of apples back to the packing shed. One or two more men hauled apples to town in the road truck. The rest worked as pickers.

Now picking, that's where the money was. If you were good at it, you could make three dollars a day. That's one hundred bushels! You started while the trees and grass are still wet, handling a twenty-foot wooden ladder. Your shoes got wet but they were mostly dry by dinner time when you ate your sandwiches. After dinner, you picked apples until dark.

The pickers were given tickets with numbers which they stuck in each crate picked. The tickets were collected as the boxes were picked up and taken to the packing shed. These tickets were collected in a locked box and taken in each night when they were sorted and tallied by my father and I or whoever else would help.

My mother worked in the packing shed while at the same time she filled up the house with boarders from the extra workers. She did the laundry and still had three meals a day for the family and the boarders.

As I would come home from the school bus, I would go directly to the packing shed and stay there until quitting time at six o'clock. I would get cold and found the best way to keep warm was to crawl into the big shredded paper boxes. One evening when the farm truck was backed up to the platform, I put a box on the truck and crawled inside and closed the flaps for the ride home. I guess my brother was trying to scare me and gave me the ride from hell over rough orchard roads, water brakes and rocks. I just rolled up in a ball, inside the box, and bounced around. Then there was a crash and I was tumbling. When I stopped, I was sealed up in the box crumpled around me. Then my brother pulled the box apart and said, "Gimmie, are you all right? Are you hurt?"

I wasn't hurt at all. The box had been the perfect cushion. I wasn't even scared because I didn't know what had happened. In my brother's zeal, he bounced the sideboard off the truck. It crashed onto the road, followed by me in the box, which tumbled over and over down across the orchard. My parents were following in the car and saw what happened They were scared!

Third and Fourth Grades

Then it was the third grade, upstairs on the right, with Miss Flowers. I don't remember much about that year except one day, in the spring, when it was warm enough to let the fire in the stove go out during the day, I began to feel sick and couldn't stop shivering. The teacher said I could go outside and since I was cold, I could sit in her car. The car seemed warm at first, and I sat with my head on the steering wheel. As I studied the things on the dash, I thought, "Hey, I got out of school." But that didn't help much because I really did feel sick. As the sun shifted around behind the school building, I began to get cold again and started shivering. I went back inside and said I was cold. She had one of the boys rebuild the fire and I leaned against the cover around the stove until the bus came.

The walk home was very hard. I got so tired. My mother said I had a fever and she put me to bed. I still felt cold. She told my father I was real sick and she wanted a bed in the living room. A bed was set up by the stove and I was moved in.

I was tired and groggy. When I'd fall asleep, I'd see funny images like cartoons and I'd giggle and laugh and wake myself with my mother holding me and saying, "It's all right." This went on through the night.

The next day my father went for the doctor. When the doctor came, he said they should keep a kettle of water boiling on the stove and that they should put dry poultices on my chest day and night. My mother made small cloth bags and my father filled these with wheat bran from the granary. These were heated on the stove and replaced as they would cool off.

The next days were a fog of waking and sleeping and lapsing into delirium. Then at some hour of some night the fever broke and I began to sweat. I had double pneumonia. This was before antibiotics, so it had been quite serious. The doctor came again and said I was getting better.

I got better slowly. I was very weak. They bought me bakery bread, bottles of pop and a six pack of RC cola. The pack of RC cost twenty-five cents and it was the first I'd ever seen. By the time Mother would let me go outside, it was warm again and over a month had passed. It was near the end of the school year so I didn't go back. I knew I'd have to go back next year. I didn't want to think about it.

My mother and sister would visit back and forth to help each other with gardening and canning. At my sister's, she would keep both Eugene and I fully busy but at my house there was usually some time for us to play. One of the games we invented was "building roads".

There was an erosion ditch under the north eave of the shed. Using an old kitchen knife, or any other piece of metal, we'd scrape out ways along one side of the bank, making a loop back along the other bank. We'd make fills, dams, bridges, whatever that day's terrain required. We would then push our little cars around the route but the principle interest was the construction. The terrain would change each time it rained and we'd have to repair it or make a new route.

Eugene Haines

Another group effort was berry picking. The woods below the house was a bramble of blackberry and raspberry bushes. I guess my father had asked, but we treated the berries like they were our own. We would pick several gallons over the few days they were ripe. My mother and sister would can some and make jelly and jam from the rest.

Summers

The shed across the road from the house was the center of much of my attention during the summer. The second story was used to store apple barrels, crates and baskets as overflow from the bigger packing shed out in the orchard. It had sliding doors at each end for loading and unloading. The lower story was built into the hill so that trucks could unload directly into the uphill end. The other end was a full two stories and the door looked out on the area between the house and corn crib, as well as toward the line of trees on the west side of the garden. The only other access to the second floor was a ladder of two-by-fours spiked to the vertical center post that led to a top door.

The lower level housed my father's blacksmith shop. It had a dirt floor, concrete walls and two small windows on the north side. There was a platform under the windows set up on saw horses to keep the bags of spray material (lime, arsenic, blue stone, etc.) off of

the damp floor. The forge was in the center, and nearby, the anvil was mounted on a tree stump. There was
another raised platform in the back corner.

To me, all of this space under these platforms
and the two shelves along the right wall inside the
door were a treasure of novel and fascinating mechanical things. Most were odd bits and pieces that were
saved for some possible future use. The upper shelf
had some supplies and some special tools. The lower
shelf, or work bench, had a collection of tools with a
vise at the end near the door. There was a saw, a
square and a drawknife hung on pegs on the side wall.

There was, I think, an unstated understanding
that I leave my father's tools alone. But my interpreta-
tion was, "Be careful, don't break anything, and don't
get caught." With the vise and the saw I learned to cut
wood without doing much damage to the saw or myself. The drawknife is a large steel bar sharpened on
one side to a keen edge with wooden handles, at an
angle, on each end.

I had seen my father use the drawknife to cut
down a piece of hickory to fit the rings and hooks to
make a singletree for the wagon.[17] The drawknife
could cut down a piece of wood to the shape you
needed. It hung on a peg on the wall, but as I shifted

---

[17] A single tree is a wooden bar used on wagons to balance the pull of
horse as it shifts weight from one shoulder to the other.

the wood in the vise, I would bump into the drawknife. Since the bench was covered with tools, so I leaned the drawknife against the base of the vice.

One day, I accidentally knocked over the drawknife and it fell on my bare left foot! It was a deep two-inch gash across the ligaments of my toes. It got infected and took a long time to heal. The toes were numb and stiff when it healed. The toes did recover but it took years.

By far the most interesting thing on the work bench was the Hot Shot. This was a 6-volt battery made up of four telephone dry cells. It was used to start the tractor each day. The old Fordson's coils were powered by the low voltage AC magneto. With the drag from transmission grease, it was nearly impossible to crank the engine fast enough to get enough voltage to fire the plugs. So, the Hot Shot was substituted for the magneto to start the engine, then disconnected and put back on the bench. You could get shocked when you transferred the wires so I was never permitted to do this but I watched.

When you touched the wires from the Hot Shot together, this produced sparks. I knew this would run down the battery so it was only done briefly to contemplate the possibilities.

My favorite pastime was taking things apart to see how they worked. I would usually put them back together, but sometimes I would decide an item was more useful to me and I would keep it, or some part of it, and modify it for my own use. I found that inside a Model-T horn was an electromagnet that would pull in the metal diaphragm when the Hot Shot was connected. I could make a headphone. It was the size and weight of a wind up alarm clock but with a metal band bent to fit around the head. Attached to one of the bolts, it was a kind of headphone.

We had a hand crank, floor model Victrola that had been bought ten or twelve years before for my sister. I could only remember us buying one record in my life time. It was kept in the summer parlor or in a spare room. Any thing I would do with it, I would have to do in secret.

I set out to build an electric reproducer that would play a record through my headphone. I made the arm out of wood with metal strips tacked to the sides to make bearing surfaces for both the horizontal and vertical pivots. I drilled a large vertical hole in the end of the arm and pivoted a U-shaped piece of tin with a piece of cork in the end to hold the needle. This was spring loaded by a rubber band. I then drilled an intersecting hole into the end and inserted a nut for an adjustment screw to touch the pivot. I didn't understand that the sound pattern on the record was cut across the record instead of into the record like Edison's original tin foil model. So, my design was all wrong.

Then one day, when no one was home, I took the Hot Shot and headphone up to the Victrola and hooked it up. By fiddling with the adjustment screw, I could get sound through the headphone for seconds at a time. I was elated but this was the best it would do. Now, I understand why it was intermittent, but I didn't then.

Occasionally, we made what seemed like safari trips to what my parents called "the land back on the mountain." This was our land beside my father's childhood home, where he had cleared the orchard so we could plant another garden. There was a small creek within hiking distance and I would spend as much time as I could get away with wading in the pools and digging under the rocks. There were tadpoles, minnows, and crayfish.

One time there were salamanders. I caught several and brought them home. Now, I had to have a pond to put them in. I dug a small pit in the yard and carried water to fill it. I put in the salamanders but the water kept seeping out. This wouldn't work.

I knew I could siphon water out of the tank at the well and I wondered if I could get water up to the pond. I got together all the old spray hose I could find. It didn't reach by four feet. I found a couple of sections of old bent pipe.   My connections were makeshift. They leaked, but the water would just rise to fill the pond.

The salamanders didn't seem to really like the water and kept climbing out on the bank.   Then it was evening.   The next morning they were all gone, I never saw any of them again.

Although I had neatly buried the hose in the yard, the hose and pipe were across the road, so I had to put it all away the next day.   It bugs me now, that I didn't see the obvious from this experience.   If I could siphon water to ground level in the yard, water would have flowed into the basement, like into a barrel. Even if I had to straighten the pipe and buy connections, with a barrel of water in the basement, I would only have had to carry it upstairs.   Or, I could have talked my father into buying a pump.   Oh, for missed opportunities.

My father would have two or three barrels of cider made each fall.   As was the custom, he would have it put in new whisky barrels and in a few weeks it would begin to develop its own alcohol.   One Sunday, the men were sampling the batch and my brother brought an iced tea pitcher into the back room.   He managed to start a contest between Eugene and I to see who could drink more glasses.   After a while we were staggering around in the backyard.   I don't remember it very well but I know my mother spanked me with a switch. It didn't hurt. I fell asleep and woke up sick. I didn't do that again.

My brother George continued attending school in Bunker Hill. He had to walk a long way to meet the bus and began begging my father to get him a car. After George had saved some of the money, he and my dad went to Washington, D.C. and bought a two-year-old, '34, two door, Ford V8 from a used car lot. In the fall he drove this to school.

During my brother's senior year at high school, the principal organized a trip for some of the boys to see the Chesapeake Bay east of Baltimore. He came back with stories so strange they could hardly be believed. There was a body of water, so wide, you couldn't see the other side. There was white sand all along the shore and the water was salty. There were waves that could knock you down, or turn over a boat. The group had gone out fishing and had been caught in a sudden storm, they had broken an oar and almost didn't get back. My brother had to take the family back to see this.

We couldn't talk my father into going, but my mother, brother, sister, brother-in-law, nephew, and I all set out to see the bay. For some part of the trip, my mother fretted because my father hadn't come. Finally, in a very adult tone, my brother told her, "He had his chance to come. He didn't come, so you enjoy yourself. I don't want to hear any more about it." She took the advice.

My brother George knew where to go and what to do. There was a farmer that would let you park in his field by the beach for a fee. We stayed a couple of days, ate the food we had brought with us and slept on the grass and in the car. My brother and brother-in-law Ruble rented a boat and went fishing. Eugene and I played in the sand, collected shells, climbed over the big green row boats, waded in the water and got knocked down by the waves. It was all he had said it would be, it was great.

**Glen's brother-in-law
Ruble Haines**

I dreaded going back to school. I had been home with pneumonia at the end of the last school year and I hadn't gotten my report card. On the first day I found a seat in the third grade section. After the room had settled down and the teacher had looked us over, she called me up to her desk and gave me my report card.

She said I should be sitting in the fourth grade side. I was pleased but also scared. I felt I had fallen behind. I didn't think I could keep up.

The only subject I can remember now was long division. I caught on to the mechanics of the operation and those hours of flashcard drills paid off. I could remember enough of my multiplication tables to get by. Then, there was my classmate Delbert. By the time Delbert learned long division, all of the third grade could do it.

There was a new boy in class, he was rough and enjoyed playing the bully. He looked for every opportunity to call me a sissy. This was very easy on the playground. All the boys were suppose to play baseball. I couldn't hit the ball and I couldn't catch the ball. My brother had tried to teach me but when I got hit in the face with a green apple that bloodied my nose, he gave up. My solution was to volunteer to play umpire. I say "play" because I didn't know how to do that either. I didn't know the rules. I got a "Big 5" scratch pad and designed a form to keep score. I did learn enough, finally, to just assume I'd be umpire. It was a struggle.

In the summer that followed, my interest in the Hot Shot persisted. My brother said he knew how to send messages through a wire. He wouldn't tell me how, only saying, "You get some wire and I'll send a message from one end to the other."

"You mean like from upstairs to downstairs?"

"Yeah, if you get the wire."

Without actually demolishing anything, I found bits and pieces of wire and pieced them together to run from the room on the hall landing, out the window, over the porch roof and in the door to the top of the ice box down stairs. When my brother came in from work I showed him I had the wire.

He went to the shed got the Hot Shot and a Model-T coil. He put the coil upstairs and the Hot Shot downstairs. When he hooked up the battery downstairs the coil upstairs buzzed. He said messages were sent by dots and dashes that represented letters. This was telegraph. I knew that. I felt cheated. This did, however, start me on collecting a length of good wire.

Over that year at school, I had discovered the encyclopedia in the seventh/eighth grades room. I'd been able to sneak in at recess and look up things like "telephone" and "radio". It didn't tell you how it worked, but it showed you pictures of all of this including Edison's carbon transmitter. It was a little round button with a small bolt and nut on one side.

I had taken apart old telephone batteries and the center post was carbon and the brass cap at the end had a little bolt and a nut. So I sawed off the top of one of these posts, leaving the piece of carbon in the brass cap, and then ground the carbon smooth on the grind stone. It looked just like the picture.

Then, continuing this look-alike search, I found donut-shaped rings in quart cans of Cup Grease. They were shiny, with turned over edges. Two of these placed together back to back looked like a microphone. So I mounted a metal plate, set off by foam rubber between the donuts and attached the carbon button so it could be adjusted to touch the plate through the hole on one side.

By this time, I had made a much smaller headphone from the innards of an auto horn and the case of an ammeter. With the Hot Shot and very careful adjustment of the carbon button, it was a one way telephone. My big problem was having no "Watson". I could only test it when family came to visit and there was enough confusion to sneak the Hot Shot into the attic.

It amazes me now, that I never understood Edison's carbon mike. If I had crushed the carbon into little pebbles, they would have been self adjusted by gravity and would have worked much better. Then, if I had understood the high impedance headphone and the induction coil, I would have made a real one-wire telephone. Oh, the ignorance of youth.

One time, on one of those many running trips to

steal the Hot Shot, I dropped it from the work bench on to my left bare foot. Yes, it landed about half an inch from the scar left by the cut from the summer before. The battery had a sharp edge and it, too, cut my foot. It became infected, and took a long time to heal.

By this time my mother had extensive flower beds in her chicken-protected yard. My brother had gotten an old push lawn mower somewhere and I could now mow the backyard (which we used as a frontyard). What had grown, on its own, was not grass, it was a little low weed with two tiny leaves, but it was green, and it looked neat when it was cut.

The "front" yard had grass but it had grown into clumps and I couldn't get the push mower through these. My brother would mow it with a scythe every now and then.

My standard chores remained weeding the garden, carrying water, carrying wood, helping with canning and big Sunday dinners. One day, Uncle Harry came to visit, cases of beer were bought and put on ice and there was a noisy party for a whole night.

Apple Butter

One of the family/community efforts each fall was making apple butter. It was made outdoors in a copper lined iron kettle over an open fire. The process started by finding when you could borrow the kettle from a neighbor. Then, on the evening before the event, family and neighbors were invited to cut apples.

The apples had to be peeled, cored, and quartered and it took several bushels to make the twenty-five gallons, or so, which was a typical batch. There would be one or two mechanical apple peelers, borrowed and clamped to the table. Operating one of these was my preferred job. The apple core was placed on the prongs of a shaft and, as you turned the crank, the apple rotated and a blade, held against the apple by a spring was rotated through a half circle to cut the peeling off as a ribbon. The apple then went to the hand operation of being cut into quarters and the bit of core on each was cut away.

This evening was also a social event. There was gossip while we worked, and cake, pies and coffee after the job was completed.

In the morning, the copper-clad kettle was set up in the yard. It was washed out and then a couple of buckets of water was dumped in before the fire was built. You had to know your neighbor very well to

trust him with this kettle because the inner surface could be ruined if it was overheated.[18]

Bushels of apples were then added to make a stirrable mixture. The stirrer was a large wooden paddle mounted vertically to a long horizontal pole as a handle. The end of the paddle was rounded so it would slide over and cover all parts of the curved copper bottom.

As the water in the first mix would cook down, more apples were added until it looked like apple sauce. The cooking went on all day with continuous

---

[18]Image: Apple Butter Preparation; Carrie Lupton Bond, 163-34 wfchs, Walker Bond Family Papers, Stewart Bell Jr. Archives, Handley Regional Library, Winchester, VA

and careful stirring, passed from one person to the next, to keep the mixture from sticking to the bottom.

At some point, the old-timers knew when it was time to add the sugar. They used a lot of sugar, which was poured from a hundred pound bag. When the color was just the right shade of amber, the fire was pulled out and the butter was dipped into fruit jars and gallon crocks, which had been washed and set out during the day. The last step, after the butter had cooled, was to melt paraffin wax and cover the top of each container.

Fifth Grade

The next year I went to the fifth grade in Miss Funk's room across the hall. The most significant thing I remember about that year was her reading *Tom Sawyer* and *Huckleberry Finn* to the class. This was done the last thing of the day and depended on how well she thought we had done our class work. It was what I looked forward to and even with my slow reading, in the years to come I read most of Twain's books. He was my intellectual hero.

My hill, that swept up from the house in the green-grass summer, was a very different thing in winter. It had to be climbed first thing, on the way to the school bus. The wind always came from the west and it was an aching cold-in-the-face wind. For a couple of years I had the kids aviator's helmet with the metal rimmed plastic goggles snapped up across the forehead and the droopy hound ear flaps that would snap under the chin. When the goggles were down, it helped, but they would fog up.

Glen in his aviator hat with his nephew Eugene Haines

Once over the hill, the orchard hills and woods were protection from the wind and it wasn't so bad.

There must have been some days when the bus couldn't get around, but I don't remember any snow days. There would have been no way to know if school was closed.

There were many days when the school ground was covered with snow and you had to cross it to go to the toilet. The big boys would wait behind the corner of the back wall and pelt us with snowballs on the way. One day we decided to fight back. That day there were more small kids than large, and it wasn't a very even fight. The principal, seeing this, joined in on the side of the big boys. Now, this was an opportunity no school kid could miss and immediately all of our snowballs were directed at the principal.

I don't think he had thought this through. It was still in fun, but he retreated back down the driveway where there wasn't much snow, but there was ice. He slipped and fell and ripped his pants. He got up and tried to recover his dignity, but on review, he disappeared down the road to the house where he rented a room.

He was a sorry sight retreating down the road with a slit in the seat of his pants. It didn't even occur to us to follow him off the school ground. We went back inside. After the initial glee, we were not at all sure what the consequences would be. We went back to our rooms without saying anything to our teachers. Things went on as usual. I worried for several days that there would be some repercussions. There were none. I don't remember the boys ambushing us again, though.

I had learned to drive the farm truck by moving it from stop to stop while we hauled in the hay. That wasn't my first attempt, my brother had let me drive his car part way home once. I failed to stop at the first gate and smashed into it. It broke the gate but didn't do any lasting damage to the car. We didn't admit it. My father repaired the gate and I think he knew.

This year my father decided he could let me

drive the tractor for the spray rig. It went fine until we hit our first flat rock ledge in the orchard. The tractor's drive wheels had steel bar cleats. If one wheel hit a flat rock surface, an inch below the sod, and this was not uncommon in the Shenandoah blue limestone, the wheel would spin, bouncing on the cleats.

To get off the ledge, you had to depress the clutch, back up, and pick a different path. But control of the clutch on a Fordson was not for a skinny twelve year old. I had to put both feet on the clutch petal and my shoulder under the steering wheel to get it stopped. If my feet had slipped off the steel petal, I would have gone under the cleats of the jumping wheel. When I got it stopped, my father said, "No, you'll have to wait until you're older."

That summer, there was more work that I could do. I helped nail acid bands around apple trees for insect control. I replanted missing corn and helped weed and hoe in a section of the

SCHOOL DAYS

1938·39

Glen, age 11

field over run by grass. This was still at ten cents an hour, but that was a dollar a day. That gave me some money.

I found there were light bulbs that looked like the household variety but would burn from 6-volt batteries, which was the voltage of auto batteries at that time. I bought a 25-watt and a 50-watt. The dry cells in the Hot Shot would not fully light either bulb.

My brother George said he knew where we could get a generator. There was an abandoned truck in a neighbor's field. We took the generator off, but it was odd. It was driven by the flywheel and thus had only a cogged gear on the end of the shaft. I found I could clamp a Model-T fan pulley to this gear with the four bolts over the edge. I then rigged a belt from the hand crank drive of the forge, and with this I could spin the generator. I could light either light bulb, but I was amazed how hard it was to turn. It was nothing you could do for very long.

When the big house was built, a spring house was an essential part of the family farm because it provided the only available refrigeration. Now this natural resource had been taken over by the excesses of mechanized spraying. There had once been a large stone spring house, but now, only part of one wall and the end were standing. They had become part of the barnyard fence. The spring/well still did overflow in the early spring. The water flowed out toward the spring house wall and then, somehow, reappeared from the stone wall under one side of the corncrib. It flowed past the garden and across the hay field and then into the woods. As soon as spraying began we used three thousand gallons of water a day and the water would slow and then cease.

The basement of the house was very deep with a dirt floor. It was cool but not enough to keep milk all day in summer. We had an old, open top, ice box and would buy ice from time to time or would keep what was left over when we made ice cream with my sister's family.

In summer we'd make ice cream about once a week at one house of the other. The visitor would bring the ice. It took less than fifty pounds, at twenty-five cents, to make two-and-one-half gallons of ice cream. We always had the milk and cream and the eggs to make a cooked custard mix. We could always make chocolate or vanilla, but in season we made strawberry, peach or raspberry ice cream. Sometimes, we would buy a can of maple walnut flavoring. This was my favorite, it cost about twenty-five cents.

When the women had made the mix, we'd chip in the ice, add salt and turn the crank until it was hard to turn. By this time, it was usually dark. We'd sit around the porch and eat the ice cream and talk. After eating our ice cream, we kids, who were still without shirts and shoes, would begin to get cold. We'd curl up on the porch swing under any cover we could find. My sister's little, all black dog, called Snowball, was a welcome bed fellow. We would go home about eleven o'clock.

Oak icebox with brass hinges

Then, one of our cousins by marriage got a summer job delivering ice around the country. He volunteered to bring us ice each week. This meant two miles off his route and through two gates. He had to stop, open, pull through, and close each gate. He also helped us find an ice box for the kitchen, the kind with oak panels and brass hinges and latches. Now, we had cold milk and ice water right there in the kitchen.

During that summer, George invited one of the stores to bring out a radio on a free trial basis. Men came out and put up an antenna from the house to the smokehouse and installed it in the living room. But in summer, the parlor was seldom used. This had been done without my father's approval, and after a week, they came and took it back.

After the years with chickens, my mother had decided she wanted to raise turkeys on a large scale. These would need a yard to run in, so my father worked an arrangement with his boss and built a fenced-in area in the pasture. This was on one side but near the top of my hill. With his own lumber, he built a

Philco radio was maintained in pristine condition in Glen's home in Joppa, MD

small house, which you could walk through, but it could still be moved. The turkeys required constant cleaning, feeding and watering. I hauled water up the hill in two lard cans in my wagon. When the turkeys were sold and the feed bill paid the profit was split with the boss and my father.

By the third year of this, my mother demanded a larger split and that she should have some say in how the money was spent. So, in the fall of '39, we got a "No Squat, No Squint" slant-front, Philco floor model radio. The radio cost seventy dollars, which was nearly all of the turkey money that year.

It used a 1.5-volt A battery and a 90-volt B battery which came in a pack and cost nine dollars. The battery would last about a year, but the volume wasn't very loud over the last month. (For its purpose, it was a very good radio and although, at one point, I replaced its innards with electric parts, through what would qualify as archeology, it has been restored and is working in my basement with its original battery parts.)

Like most farm houses, our kitchen was the center of the family's activity during fall and winter. The wood stove burned all day proving warmth and the smell of fresh baking and simmering food. There was a long, oilcloth-covered table and bench along the wall that always had the best lamp in the house (maybe the only lamp). This was the comfort of the kitchen.

The parlor was seldom heated, and even when it was, it was too formal to be comfortable. Now, the radio was in the parlor and making this into a winter living room took some doing. The prized Brussels rug was taken upstairs away from the wood burning stove, The leatherette furniture, that had always been cold to the touch, had to be covered.

I had learned to use my mother's sewing machine at about eight. At first, it was the only way I could look inside and figure out how it worked. Then my mother was making quilt squares, and I could do that.

I wanted my mother to recover the two chairs and maybe the sofa. We bought the fabric. I found the chairs could be unbolted and taken apart. We put a layer of cotton batting over the Leatherette and with my mother doing some of the sewing and me doing the tacking, it went very well.

The radio now gave the family something in common to do on the long winter evenings. This, of course, took me from my homework, but I told myself, and my parents, that I could study and listen to the radio, too. In addition, I built model airplanes, model boats, and a soap carving of the Jefferson Memorial as a school project.

Having the radio created a new element of friction between my mother and me. Just at the time I got home from school, there were radio serials. I think I listened to four, but *Jack Armstrong* is the only one I can remember, now. They were each 15 minutes in length. That's 5 minutes for commercials, 3 minutes to recount yesterday's cliffhanger, which left 7 minutes to work through the plot to the next cliffhanger. The plot moved very slowly, but I didn't think I could miss an episode. This annoyed my mother because there was the wood and the water to be carried. "And it's gonna get dark!" she'd insist.

I would always do these chores, even if it did get dark, but my mother would have to remind me several times during the hour. "Now, it's gettin' dark, and you have to get in the wood." Calmly explaining that I considered this my responsibility, and that I would do it, didn't help.

One of the major problems with not having electricity, was lighting the house at night. It was cus-

tomary to have a kerosene lamp in the kitchen, one in the living room and one to carry with you as you went to bed. But the straight wick kerosene lamp is like a 10-watt bulb. You had to be a foot away to read.

The same cousin who delivered ice was now selling Al-

Aladdin lamp with its mantle created the equivalent of a 60-watt bulb

addin lamps. These were kerosene, too, but had a tubular wick, maybe four times as large as the straight wick, and this heated an asbestos mantle which converted the blue red flame to a brilliant white. This was like a sixty watt bulb. It was a godsend.

Next, he sold kerosene irons. A little tank could be filled through the handle, pumped up, and heated with an alcohol torch to start the evaporation. Once I started it for her, my mother could iron for hours with no cord or trips to the stove to reheat the flatirons. My mother loved it.

Sixth Grade

For its time and age, the school in White Hall had been built with some degree of planning for flexibility. Downstairs, the two walls of the central hall were folding doors which could be opened to make the whole lower floor into one room. This was done for public meetings and for the Christmas program. At these times, a stage was set up on saw horses in the first-grade room.

One time there was a traveling show family named the Pickerings. They arrived in the afternoon in two cars with two trailers, one small and one larger. I had never seen a vehicle that you could live in. It was a thing of exotic wonder to imagine traveling around and being in a new place each day.

At recess, "beings" came out of these strange things. The adults were busy going from trailer to trailer but there was a little girl that talked to some of the school girls and actually walked around the school house with them.

The show that night was like nothing we had ever seen before. Real people, that sang and danced and played horns, guitars and banjos. They changed and played different instruments right on the stage. They all knew their parts perfectly and went right from one thing to the next. It was amazing. It was magic.

Rumors of what the girl actually said were whispered among the girls the next day, and the boys, off by themselves, made rude remarks as to what they could do to "that".

The Pickerings had made it look so easy and fun. We had to put on a show. Miss Funk liked class projects and she listened to our proposal. We would put on something like a radio show. We'd put a sheet over the door to the storage room and everybody would do their act from that side and we'd listen in the classroom like a radio.

We asked everybody to bring in all their musical instruments. We got some toy drums and concertinas. When we asked their owners what they would play, they said, "Oh, we can't play them, you said bring them in."

"Well, can't you learn for the show?"

"No."

That ended our hopes for a band. Someone said you could tune bottles with water and play music on them. We made up a rack to hang the bottles on and, by trial and much error, came up with a one octave scale. One of the girls learned to play tunes from the song book.

So, most of our radio show was talk. I made a microphone and set it on a stick in a map stand and told anyone who would listen that it was real. It had two wires hanging out. I had bought it from a radio offer but was afraid to try to hook it up to the radio at home. The mic was mostly ignored since it wasn't hooked to anything and you couldn't see it through the sheet.

Butchering

In this era and in this way of life, butchering day was an essential function and was treated as a family and community effort. Whereas, apple butter or quilting were niceties and optional, butchering was absolutely necessary if the family was to have meat for the year. The knowledge and nuances of the art were passed down from generation to generation, as well as the livestock plan required to have animals ready to butcher at the right time of year. Preserving the meat required careful collaboration with Mother Nature. Success in the long range planning of this endeavor was a marker of the family's overall common sense and responsibility.

A number of pigs — two, three or four — according to the size of the family would be bought or raised from your own sow in the late winter or early spring. If you raised your own, then the pregnancy had to be planned before this. The pigs were fed, morning and evening for the rest of the year on the kitchen scraps and the sour milk, discarded from the day before. In the fall this would be augmented with wheat bran and corn.

In the coldest part of the winter — and this was essential to properly cure the meat — a day was chosen as butchering day. This was a matter of judgment, experience, and luck. Beyond the weather, picking the specific day was dependent on the number of family members and neighbors that could be available to help. It was a big job. Then, there was the availability of equipment, for this, too, was a community effort. Seldom did any one person own all of the needed equipment, so it was borrowed and loaned.

The scalding tank was a long wooden tank about 2 1/2 by 6 feet with a metal bottom and metal cover on the sides. It was placed over a trench dug in the ground which ended with a chimney of two or three sections of stove pipe. A fire was built in the trench and the water heated until there were some local boiling spots.

Killing the hogs was a precise, if violent, process. The hog must be shot with a 22 Long in the center of the forehead. This would cause immediate paralysis and death. Then a major artery was cut in the neck to drain all of the blood. The blood was discarded.

The carcass was then dragged to the scraping table, which was attached to one side of the scalding tank. Chains were placed under the hog as two men straddled the tank and rolled the hog into the tank. Then the men rotated the hog in the scalding tank while a third person kept testing the hair on different parts of the animal. When the condition was right, (too hot would reset the hair), the carcass was pulled out with the chains onto the table. Then using hog scrapers, which are wood handles with a little metal oval cup on one end and a larger one on the other, were used to extract, not cut, all of the hair.

When the skin was clean, the hind legs were split to expose the achilles tendons. A spreader pole was inserted under one tendon and two or three men would lift the animal and hang it on a horizontal pole using the stretcher pole under the two tendons.
The head was cut off and the carcass gutted. The liver and heart were saved. These steps were repeated for each hog.

After the bodies had cooled, each was cut into two halves, extracting the back bone. Each half was then placed on a clean table, either indoors or in an outbuilding, and separated into shoulder, ribs, tender loin (pork chops), side meat (bacon), and ham. The shoulders and hams were then rounded off to make a compact shape for curing. All of the trimmed scraps were saved, cut up and sorted for use in lard or sausage

The fat was cut into cubes and collected in a large iron pot which was fired until all of the grease was cooked out. The remains were then placed in a lard press to squeeze out all of the liquid and leave the dry cakes called crackling.

The lean scraps were run through a meat grinder to make pork sausage. If stuffed sausage was made, this was done by placing the ground and seasoned meat in the lard press, without the strainer basket, and pressing it out into the casings. Yes, the natural cas-ings were made from the small intestines of the hog. But these were not just cleaned, the two layers of tis-sue were actually separated, and only the outer layer was used. This was a delicate skill and was usually left to my mother.

Later in the day, the hearts and some other scraps were cooked in an outdoor pot. Meal and sea-soning were added to make scrapple. The hams, shoulders, and side meat were cooled overnight and then prepared to cure by either packing them in salt or by coating them with a commercial product called sugar cure mixed with white and brown sugar. These were then wrapped tightly with brown paper and hung in the smoke house. The success of the cures depended on it remaining cold for some weeks.

Over the next few days, the sausage and tenderloins were canned by my mother, with help from my sister, and maybe a visiting aunt. Small amounts of the fresh meat, that is those parts not set aside for curing, were shared among the families that came to help. There was never any money exchanged but it was expected that you would help the other family with their butchering or any other task, if they asked.

Although each piece of this equipment was privately owned, it was understood to be part of the community need. If any of the pieces were forced to be sold at public auction, it would be expected that someone, who could afford it, would buy it for continued community use. Of course, to participate, any piece borrowed, was treated carefully, and meticulously cleaned before it was returned. Anything less would be a family disgrace.

For the school system, any work excuse from your parents was valid. Butchering was the only job for which my father permitted me to stay home. I had learned to handle a .22 rifle at about the age of eight and was pretty good at targets. But guns never fascinated me and I never went hunting with my father or my brother. My father expected me to help on butchering day but he did not insist I participate in the killing phase of the task. There were plenty of other things to do.

Spring

As a class in school we had no musical instruction, except once. I remember a teacher explaining the letter names of the notes on the staff and how to tell what key a song was written in. But since I didn't know what a key was, it didn't mean much.

For some reason, the County Supervisor, who visited occasionally, thought our class could sing. We got to go to the county music festival in Winchester. It was held at Handley High School. The building was on a hill with broad white steps leading up from the athletic field that served as the backdrop for the Apple Blossom Pageant each year. Thousands of people came to see the pageant including governors, queens and princesses. That day, we had travelled there on a new bigger bus and sat in a numbered section of the audito-

Handley High School during the Apple Blossom Festival.

rium, actually, more like a theater, in a school. It was great.

I had been fascinated with cameras even as a tiny kid. I would sneak into the spare room and dig under the clothes in the dresser, take out my sister's box camera and look at it and put it back before I was caught. She had gotten this camera for the family trip to Dayton, Ohio, when I was three. She had taken a whole roll of eight pictures on the trip, on the porch at Uncle Harry's and at the air field he took us to visit. I don't remember any other pictures taken with it. I'm sure they were considered too expensive for those hard times. I eventually got up the nerve to open the back of the camera and slide out the metal box-frame on which the paper roll film was loaded. Then I would put it together and hide it away again.

Now that I could work part time in the summer, replanting corn and picking cherries, I secretly bought my own little camera. I say "secretly" because I was sure my father would not approve of me wasting my money like that. I think it cost $2.49, but that was twenty-five hours of work! It took sixteen pictures on a 2-cent roll of film, but having them developed was still too expensive, so I didn't take many pictures.

In Miss Funk's class I had more time to visit the encyclopedia in the principal's room during recess. One day he saw me studying a diagram of the innards of a camera and he offered to teach me how to develop pictures. He brought in his own equipment and taught me how to make contact prints and enlargements. Of course, I couldn't afford any equipment or even paper and developer. I thought there was a limit to how much I could bum from him.

He also brought in his camera. He said it was a 35mm camera with a 3.5f lens which had two focal ranges and a variable shutter speed. I didn't know what all that meant, so I started reading everything I could find about photography. I learned about film speed, depth of field and all that stuff. Now, I had to have a better camera!

That spring, we went on class hikes and sat under the oak trees on the school ground and read aloud. One year we did our own pageant for May Day and Jim Hutton did the announcing through the horn of an old radio speaker. He sounded just like the guy at the Apple Blossom Festival.

I never felt I had any close friends in grade school. My prime interests were things mechanical and technical, and no one else seemed to have those interests. I didn't like games. I told myself they were a waste of time, but there was the fact that I wasn't good at them. My brother tried to teach me poker, but I never got it. Card games required you to remember too many things. Then, there was a more basic problem: I just didn't have even the most benign form of killer instinct. I would feel sorry for an opponent if I won, and there was no fun in losing.

I envied the kids that lived in the village of White Hall. They could visit each other and play together on weekends. I was too far away, too isolated. On one occasion, after I got my better bicycle, I rode the five miles to White Hall and went to Jim's house. His mother said he was helping his father and told me where they were, about two miles away. I went on to the place she had directed me and found that he and his father were assembling apple barrels. We talked awhile but his father called him back. After watching how the head groves were cut in the staves, I went home.

During the summer, I bought some trays, developer, fixer, paper and a print frame to try to make some pictures, but I had no controlled light source. At one point, I rigged up the little room in the attic with black cardboard that I could raise or lower with a string to control the light from the Aladdin lamp set on a stand outside. It didn't work very well and it was too dangerous to burn the hot lamp outside the room while I worked inside.

When George's, now steady, girlfriend Virginia found how interested I was in things electrical, she had her father give me two antique RCA Radiolas. One

George Love Whitacre and Virginia Lee Miller

had two tubes and the other had four. And since tubes were the absolute latest thing when they were sold, the tubes projected through the top cover so you could adjust the heater voltage by the color of the filaments. Each took a 2-volt A battery and, probably, a 135-volt B. I used one cell of an auto battery for the A and one of the old discarded 90-volt batteries for the B. After much fiddling around I was able to receive the one local station with the headphones George had given me (these were real headphones).

Then, one day when Eugene and I were playing around with it, he attempted to shift to another cell on the auto battery but moved the wrong wire first, putting 4 volts on the tubes and burned out two of our four tubes. After that there was no hope of getting the four tube model to fully work. I took the coupling transformer out of the second stage and built a separate amplifier with other tubes. With this I could use a headphone as a microphone.

Now I set out to run a wire to the tenant house. It was a single wire and I thought it had to be well insulated. Then, (stupid, stupid, stupid), instead of spending a few cents for insulators, I cut up the two tube Radiola to use the Bakalite to make insulators. With this amplifier, I could get voice over the wire, but since it was one wire, the ground loop pickup of the 60-cycle field was deafening.

The wire was well insulated. I found that during the build up of a storm, the lead-in would shock you. Once, I hooked the wire to a neon bulb and it glowed for hours. I once showed this to my father, he thought it was some kind of trick. He couldn't believe it was coming out of the charge in the air.

It was about this time that I decided to make myself an electric soldering iron. We had a blow torch in the shed which burned gasoline, but in the few times we had tried to light it, it had behaved more like a

117

flame thrower, once setting things on fire ten feet away. I wouldn't think of trying to use it in the house.

I bought a little dime store copper iron and drilled a hole down the center from the top. I then unwound the heating element from an auto cigarette lighter and coiled it in a tight spiral to fit in the hole. I insulated it with plaster of Paris and asbestos fibers from an old iron cord. I hooked it up to the old auto battery. It worked for a while and then the element burned out. Later, my brother brought me an alcohol burner from college.

Then Summer

My brother George married Virginia Lee Miller the year he graduated from college. He came back to work on the orchard for the summer. It was decided they should have the three upstairs rooms on the south end. Two of these had been my bedroom and work room and I was moved to the 6 x 12 room on the hall landing. I decided I would paper the room. Eugene helped me. The first piece of ceiling paper started on the ceiling and finished, at the other end, half way down on the wall. We learned as we went along and we eventually got better. It worked out rather well.

Perhaps in compensation, my brother let me use a car radio he had bought as a spare, for parts. I bolted it to my iron bed. He gave me an old auto battery for it. This was one of the earliest car radios and it drew about ten amperes so it wouldn't run very long on the old battery. Now that I knew more about cameras and how to develop pictures, not having electricity was more unbearable.

I rigged a way to mount the generator so it would pivot on top of a pole. I made a two-blade and, later, an eight-blade propeller and placed them out on my hill when it was windy. Neither would turn the generator fast enough to produce power.

Later that year, I found another generator with a belt pulley and I mounted it on the platform of the engine used to pump water. This would charge about 10 amperes whenever the pump ran, which was most of the time each day. I bought wire to run from the tank tower to the attic window about 100 yards away. But not understanding wire gauge or Ohm's law, I could only get about 3 amperes to the attic. The alternative was to carry the battery to the well and then carry it back to the house for use. Now, if I had had a good battery, this would probably have worked, but what I had was an old battery that had been thrown away.

Finding a place to bathe or swim in the hot, sweaty summer was a sought after dream. The only nearby stream (maybe 10 miles) was Back Creek. It would fall to almost no flow in summer, but it still had some ponds deep enough to swim in. The family would go on some Sundays to one of these near Brannon's Ford. People came and went, but there might be twenty or thirty people swimming off of the muddy bank for most of the day.

The tank on the tower at the well was six feet deep and, maybe, six feet in diameter but the water was replaced over and over each day and most of the time was too cold to swim. After I found I could siphon water out of the tank, I patched together enough old hose to run past the old spring house ruin, over the barnyard gate and into the unused side of the corncrib. Then with a faucet from a spray gun and a clothes sprinkler head I had a shower. But once the warm water ran out of the hose, it was a shower with the same problem as the tank, it was too cold!

Then I found a long piece of 3/8 aluminum pipe which had been part of a discarded spray gun. With very much care, I was able to bend this into a coil about a foot in diameter. I set this up on a stake in the barnyard and diverted the water through the coil. Now, if you built a fire under the coil this would heat the water. Controlling the temperature was rather odd. Each fire was different and would change when you went to use the shower, the only rule, you opened the valve to get cooler water and closed it down to get hotter. Both my brother and I used this shower, it was great.

Although I had studied catalogs with cameras costing 25 and even 35 dollars, I just couldn't think I had that much to spend. Then, there in the Sears Sales Catalog, was a Marvel camera with a range finder, comparison light meter, shutter speeds of B, 1/25 to 1/200 of a second and a 3.5f lens with continuous focus. It was $9.95. It, too, was a 1/2 frame camera and would take sixteen pictures on a 25 cent roll of film. I had to have it.

By this time I was working more and I got together the money and the postage and ordered it. About a week later, I got a letter saying they were out of stock. There was a post card that asked if I wanted to cancel the order. Of course, I did not. This was followed by a series of these out-of-stock letters. I walked the mile to the mailbox to meet the mailman each time it should have come. I'd do this during my hour lunch break but sometimes the mailman was late. My father didn't like this.

Then another sales catalog came with the same camera. Now the price was $18.95 and I knew I was being strung along. I thought it must have been a mistake in the first catalog but I persisted with my "continue order" postcards. After two months of this, it finally arrived the day I helped my brother move to his teaching job in Woodstock, Va.

I helped him move into a house on a hill on the west side of town. While unloading, I opened the door to the shed behind the house and pulled down a hornet's nest onto my bare back. Several stung me. It hurt, but worse, I was allergic to honey bees, I would swell up from one sting, now I had several stings. My brother's wife, Virginia Lee, put soda on the stings. It still hurt and I worried, but these were hornets, not honey bees, and after the pain subsided there were no after effects. As some compensation, I now had my two rooms back.

Seventh Grade

There is considerable confusion in separating my memories of grades six and seven. I thought I was leaving Miss Funk's room and was off to Mr. Guthrie's room downstairs, but that year the school added a ninth grade which required Miss Funk to teach sixth and seventh grades. So, I was in Miss Funk's room for the third year in a row.

In the seventh grade she set us out on a major task to collect the history of the White Hall community. She assigned individual tasks to collect the history of specific sites drawing on the knowledge and memory of parents.

I volunteered to make a map of the community showing the location of each student's home. I enlarged a small section from a road map to a wall poster. I don't remember how I did this. I know I made a pantograph from the picture in the Sears catalog, but I think that was in High School. I probably used a grid overlay technique. I

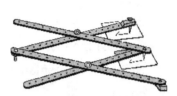

Pantagraph is an instrument used for drawing maps to scale.

remember the teacher brought in India Ink and a broad pen, it was the first time I'd worked with that. Each house was located and numbered; mine was way off in the corner.

The histories were written out on the blackboard and we were supposed to copy these and make up a notebook. I must have missed some days because my book was not complete.

We had maps that pulled down over the blackboard like window shades. One day when I was looking at the world map, I began to wonder how fast we were moving as the earth turned each day. I measured across the maps at the closest latitude and then computed the distance from the scale curve on the map. I divided this by 24 hours and got something over 900 miles an hour. No one, including myself, could quite believe this, but it had to be.

Miss Funk told me there was a science fair that spring, and she encouraged me to go with some of my things. I volunteered to take my carbon microphone and headphone, but to make these work, I needed the Hot Shot. I explained this to my father and he said I could

take it. We travelled on a big bus to the district (or maybe state) fair. I think it was held in Lexington.

At the fair I demonstrated my mic to several people, including a teacher or two, but no one told me how carbon mics were supposed to work. I didn't have it quite right, but it did function.

That year we had a school program that was a bit more mature than spelling out Christmas with spo-ken "parts" and cut out paper letters. I don't know if it was the Christmas program or something held later in the spring.

That year we had a school program that was a bit more mature than spelling out Christmas with spo-ken "parts" and cut out paper letters. I don't know if it was the Christmas program or something held later in the spring.

I was chosen to be in some kind of skit. I was

124

the husband in a long script that was mostly an argument with my wife. It was a kind of grammar school version of the radio program *Bickersons*. It was a long part and I didn't think I could learn it at first, but when I did, it was kind of fun to get into the role and have all of those people listen to you and laugh at the right spots.

White Hall School Community
by Miss Funk's Class

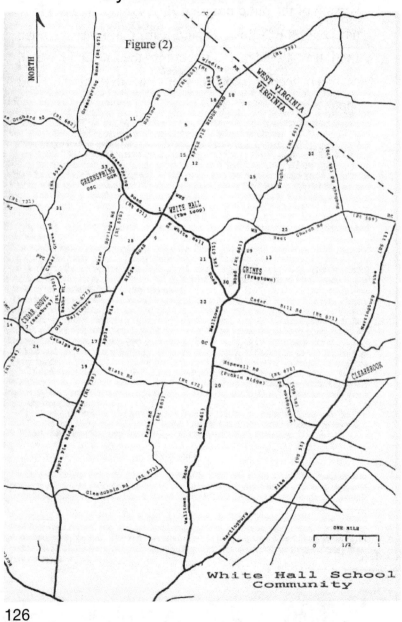

Figure (2)

Index to the numbers used to indicate the home locations of Martha Funk's sixth and seventh grade classes, 1940-1941, White Hall School, as shown on the map:[19]

Index to students' homes

1. Elizabeth Carr Anderson

2. Charles Robert Brown

3. Constance Idelia Brown

4. Delbert Combs

5. Winfred Austin Cooke

6. Dorothy Elizabeth Dellinger

7. Dora May Fries

8. Eugene Davis Funkhouser

9. Margaret Grubbs

10. James Helsley

11. Harold Loyd Hensley

12. James Vernon Hutton, Jr.

13. Charles Lawrence Kerns

14. Kenneth Pifer Lewis

15. Nancy Bruce Lodge

(9) Arbutus Morris

17. Leona Marie Murray

18. Mary Ellen Nethers

---

[19]The original map was copied on a 1940 Hectograph machine, which made the copies blue. Glen recreated the map with the help of classmate James V. Hutton in 1995. Copies of the original still exist.

19. Van Hoover Nicholson

20. Calvin Owens

21. John Doil Parsons

22. Anna Mae Rowland

23. Henry Irvin Russell

24. Alson Howard Smith, Jr.

25. Frances Smith

26. Eddie Snapp

27. Guy Dutton Snapp

28. Bennie Strother, Jr.

29. Ida Jean Taylor

30. Austin Lorraine Tusing

31. Donovan Wesley Umstot

32. Charles Glenvil Whitacre

33. Curtis Wendell Wilson

Index to places of interest

CG Galilee Church

LMC Little Mountain Church

MPC Mt. Pleasant Church

OGM Old Greenspring Mill

OSC Old Stone Church

PVC Pleasant Valley Church

RC Rest Church RH The Rock House

SR Smoke Residence

WHS White Hall School WS Woodbine School

Last Summer

By the next summer my father had modified the spray rig[20]. With the old steel-wheeled rig, a great deal of time was lost in the trips to and from the water tank to refill. Now, they had bought an old International Truck and mounted the tank, motor and pump on the frame. This would be faster on the trips back and forth to the well.

I could drive this. The clutch and gears worked well but the brakes were mechanical, operated by steel

[20] Image: Apple Spraying. "The Careful Operator", 239-13 vwfchs, Old Time Applegrowers Collection, Stewart Bell Jr. Archives, Handley Regional Library, Winchester, VA

cables. Controlling the downhill speed for the walking sprayer, and not bouncing my father around in the ring on top of the spray rig was very hard. It would cut off the circulation in my right leg and even in my back against the knobby seat. But it was a dollar a day and I could work every day.

In my spare time, I drew up plans for my darkroom. It would be 4x4x8 feet with a 2 foot door. It would be built of 1/4 inch plywood with 3/4 x 2 in. framing around each panel, arranged so it could be bolted together with overlapping joints to make it light tight. It would have an open bottom and a closed top so that it could stand alone in a room. It would have 18 in. shelves, at right angles, along two sides at desk height and a 8 in. shelf above for storage.

I bought 5 sheets of plywood, cut the frames, nailed these in place and then assembled the sides and bolted them together. When I had finished the hinges on the door, I took it all apart and reassembled it in my workroom upstairs. I completed the shelves, and then built in a print box and a 4x5 fixed enlarger, which I had made out of plywood, glass and a grapefruit juice can, using the lens from my first $2 camera.

Later, I got carried away, designing a switch panel for my darkroom. I used a red truck light on a swing arm for a safe light. I lined four switches along the bottom of the panel for three lights (and a spare

Created with a yellow photographic filter when he was about 10 years old, this was one of Glen's favorite photos

switch). Then I built a timer using the cylinder from a door check with a cocking crank and an adjustable needle valve in the air escape. I added a selector switch to change the timer from one unit to the other.

Somewhere along the way, I read about using filters to accent certain colors. I bought a yellow filter which was recommended for photographing clouds. Indeed it did, showing the clouds as billowing whites and grays against a black sky.

I photographed many pretty clouds but my favorite was a picture of my niece and the two kids from the tenant house taken from a distance on top of

131

Glen's black & white photo that he colorized by hand

my hill against a sky of clouds like the backdrop for a movie. This picture hangs in my den.

In those days, one of the drugstores sold photographic paper and chemicals. I asked them about an enlarger and they showed me one in a catalog for only $6. I ordered it. It was worth about $6. It over-heated the negatives and caused then to wrinkle. The lens was about as good as the one from my $2 camera. But with this, I could make 8x10 enlargements.

One of my favorite pictures was of a view of the lane as it wound through the rocky part of the pasture just inside the first gate. With this enlarger, and at this size, the outer edges were blurred and unclear. But I had bought a coloring kit of transparent oils and I set about coloring it. This was difficult and beyond my artistic talent but I persisted and produced a picture I could hang on the wall.

Later when I had my own home, I took the picture from the living room at my mother's. I later learned that my mother had cried about losing it so I reframed it and gave it back to her. It is now in our living room.

My sister had bought her own washing machine a few years before, and by then, Maytag had designed a two cylinder, two-cycle engine. This ran much quieter and smoother than the one-cylinder engine my mother had. When my sister moved from the orchard at White Post to Martinsburg, she now had electricity and her husband put an electric motor on the washing machine, so she offered the two cylinder engine to my mother. I made a mounting board and installed it on my mother's machine.

Now, I had the one-cylinder engine and a generator. I could make a power plant! I don't know why I didn't use the generator with the pulley that I had used with the engine at the well, maybe it wasn't mine. Instead, I set out to couple the truck generator directly to the crank shaft. The pulley end of the engine ran in the wrong direction, so it had to be coupled to the end that had the starting petal. After removing the guard, there was only about 1/4 in. of shaft exposed. I found a lock ring from the handle bars of a tricycle with a set screw. I sawed off the base to make it short enough to lock on the shaft's end. The generator had a slot in the shaft, so I made a piece of flat metal to fit in this slot and into slots I filed in the lock ring. I had made a frame from two-by-fours to match the mounting arms of the engine and to hold a vertical mount I would build for the generator.

Then, I did a very dumb thing. I guess I was trying to see if the lock ring would hold. I tried to hold the generator with one hand and start the engine with my foot. It started, the generator went off center, the metal coupling bent and then it all flew apart. The metal coupling went into the palm of my left hand at the base of my third finger, nearly ripping it off.

My father took me to the doctor. It was a nasty jagged tear but no bones or ligaments were cut. The doctor coated the wound with the newly discovered sulfa antibiotic. It didn't get infected. In a week or so I was back trying to retrieve the pieces and complete my power plant.

When I had built a very sturdy vertical support out of oak for the generator, it did work. I put it in the attic and ran the exhaust outside. I then fished 14 gauge wire down to the darkroom. It worked, but it was very noisy up there.

To complete the illusion, I fished wire through the wall into the big bedroom and installed a receptacle on the chair board. Then, I made up an extension cord, bought a bed lamp, and hooked it up. Of course, I couldn't use it for any length of time, I still had the same old battery at the other end. But I could reach up and pull the chain, and I had light. It gave me a whole new sense of sophistication.

The New School

In the fall of 1941, the district's first public high school opened in Clearbrook. Up until that time, none of public schools in the Stonewall school district extend ed through the upper grades. To attend high school families either had to pay tuition or travel outside of the district. Some would even board at distant schools like Middleton. From the history that my classmate Jim Hutton has compiled, the long-range planners, (who were the movers and shakers of the community), fought against the new school being operated as a high school.[21] Their plan seemed to be to delay and delay, looking to some much larger county-

---

[21] *The Maroon and Gray in Colorful Times: A History of Stonewall High School Clearbrook Virginia* by James V. Hutton, Jr; self published.

Stonewall High School

wide high school somewhere over the horizon.

Now the city residents and wealthier county residents could attend the privately endowed Handley High School. The county residents were required to pay tuition and there was no public transportation. My brother's theory was that the wealthy orchard owners, including the Byrds, had the long range objective of protecting their supply of cheap labor, which, of course, should not be "overly educated".

So, I don't know who actually decided the new school was a high school, but the eighth and ninth grades were accepted and then moved on to graduation in the coming years. And then, we insisted on calling ourselves a high school.

I was still picked up by the same bus and taken to White Hall, but then another bus took us to high school back in Clearbrook. Later in the year, my brother helped me clear a path across the old woods so I could walk to meet the bus that went directly to Clearbrook. But the kids on this bus were all in grade school so I preferred to take the bus to White Hall most of the time.

Glen, age 15

The building was new and clean and huge, by my frame of reference. It had a permanent stage, an auditorium, central heating, and restrooms. But because all of the smaller grade schools had now been closed, these students were bussed to the new building and it was very crowded. The space planned for a cafeteria was soon converted to class rooms, the auditorium had no seats and should also have served as a gymnasium but it was too small for basketball. There were no showers for athletics, well, at least not at first. Still, it was a great school. Typing class was held in a converted hallway and the school paper was published from the auditorium stage. It was a great school.

One gray December day, I was home alone on a

Sunday afternoon. I was listening to the radio and they began interrupting programs for special announcements. Pearl Harbor had been attacked by the Japanese. Where was Pearl Harbor? It was in Hawaii; it was our Naval base. But the Japanese? I was sure it was a mistake — it was the Chinese or somehow the Germans. The Japanese just made firecrackers and cheap paper prizes for Cracker Jacks. Zeros, airplanes? I didn't belicve it.

A strange thing happened that fall. A man in his 40's came to the house one day and asked for a job. He said he has from New York and just needed to make a little money. He looked rather shabby and, I think, he had only one change of clothes. He was given a job picking apples and mother agreed to provide room and board.

In a couple of weeks, a woman, about his age, arrived by taxi from Winchester. He said she was his wife. She was wearing an old fur jacket that looked scruffy and was ripped along a seam. I wondered why she hadn't sewed it up. She stayed for a weekend and then left. The next week he was caught switching apple tickets in the filled crates in the orchard and was fired. It seemed so obvious, almost as though he wanted a reason to leave.

To us, New York meant gangsters, and we thought he might be "on the lamb" for something he had done and was hiding out. But why here, away from town and off of all the main roads?

Then as time went by, I began to think....it was 1941 — we were at war. That long wire over the hill to the tenant house was a good antenna. I had hooked a spark coil to it and played with dots and dashes to see if I could hear them on the radio. I could. Was I being checked out as an enemy transmitter? Oh, the imagination of children!

Memories of White Hall and Stonewall[22]

by Glenvil Whitacre (class of '46)

Preface

As I have tried to describe my school days, what I see on the page falls short of what I mean and what I feel. I guess our memories of school, like other childhood memories, hold a magic that is only real from that special vantage point in time. You had to have been there. The best that I can do is to try to set the scene by describing where we came from. We came by different routes but the one I can describe is my own, through Woodbine and White Hall. The events recounted are personal and, thus, very self-centered, but I hope this can at least indirectly, describe the setting in Frederick County schools in the 30's and 40's.

---

[22] This was originally written for Stonewall High School Reunion and then later published in *In and Around the Loop (Northern Frederick County, Virginia) by James V. Hutton, Jr.*. Iberian Publishing Company, Athens Georgia, 1998. It has been lightly edited for this edition.

Woodbine and White Hall

I started school at Woodbine School. I walked about two miles across the fields and joined neighbor kids at each house along the way. The third house had several kids and the mother would invite us into the warm kitchen while the kids assembled. Yes, there was snow sometimes but no one was barefoot. In fact, I had heavy high buckle galoshes and, like most of the kids, I wore knee socks and corduroy nickers that swished when you walked.

Woodbine was a one-room school with one teacher, eight grades and no well. I was only there a year in what was called the "primer". Most of what I remember came from what happened in the classes above me. There was geography, history, and spelling. Not that I learned to spell, but there were so many new words that I didn't hear at home and each was used in a sentence. It was very interesting.

The next year a bus was available to take us to White Hall School and the bus stop was only about a mile from home. I attended White Hall from the first through the seventh grades.

The school at White Hall was a two-story, frame building, covered with smooth white stucco. There were eight grades in four classrooms, each with a stove. There was a well in the yard and outhouses on the hill. The two downstairs rooms were separated by folding doors from a large central hall. This hall later became the second grade room with one wall open to the first grade room since the hall had no stove.

Once or twice a year, when special programs were planned, the other wall was folded back to make the lower floor into one big room. Large sections of floor were carried up from the coal cellar and placed on saw horses in the first grade room to form a stage. The curtains were sheets hung on a wire across the room, and the lights were the two naked bulbs from the ceiling of the first grade room. The two-foot rise of the saw horses brought the bulbs down to about adult eye level on the stage. At Christmas, the teachers brought in large clear bulbs and one time, I remember, blue bulbs for special effects on the angles.

There were good memories of simple, first-time things. When the weather was warm enough, we lined up outside to wash our hands for lunch. The water was dispensed from an old water cooler set on the edge of the back porch. One student held the button for each student and another sprinkled soapy water from a jelly jar with holes punched in the lid. The soap mixture was made by shaving a bar into water. The teacher would ask us to bring in a new bar when we could.

The town of White Hall had two general stores, one at the crossroads, and one two houses east. If the teacher needed something from the store or you could convince your teacher and the principal of a valid need, you could get permission to walk to the store along the public road during recess. I had never been chosen for one of these missions, but one day I figured if I could get money from my father for soap, this would be a valid reason.

I explained the teacher's announcement to my father and he gave me a nickel to buy the soap. I got the required permission and was off the school ground, along the public road, with the new freedom of visiting a store on my own. I stopped at the store to the east, but the door was locked. It was run by an old woman, and I had heard that if the door was locked, you went next door and knocked. Once I did, she came in through the back of the store and opened the door for me. There was an all-glass counter with brightly colored penny candy that held my attention as she went around the counter.

"How much is soap?" I asked.

"What kind you want? Octagon Laundry Soap is 8 cents and Ivory Soap is 5 cents."

"Do you have anything cheaper?" I asked, glancing toward the candy.

"No."

"OK, I'm sorry." I left.

I went to the other store. This was a brown cave

of a room and the candy case was not so well lit. Unfortunately, their cheapest soap was also 5 cents. Disappointed, I bought it and took it back to school.

I think the soap incident occurred when I was in the second grade. In later years, I learned that every so often "emergencies" could be planned — a sudden need for a new tablet or pencil lead — and I always made sure I had a few extra pennies for some wondrous penny candy!

My favorite spot in the building was the left rear corner of the seventh and eighth grade room. There, on top of the bookcase, was a set of red encyclopedias. Sometimes I would sneak in at recess and see pictures of telephones and radios and all kinds of mysterious things.

My third grade teacher didn't like this. I was supposed to play baseball. "All the boys play baseball." I was no good at baseball, and my classmates reminded me of that very often. Kenny, the class bully, was always one of the team captains. One day as the captains alternately selected players, to "choose up sides", the last turn was Kenny's and the last pick was me.

"I'll be the umpire," I blurted out in an effort to save my dignity.

He looked at me in disbelief. He thought it was a joke, but I didn't laugh. "OK," he said finally.

The only hitch in my face-saving plan was that I didn't know the rules of baseball.

I learned from experience. Experience that consisted entirely of listening to the arguments that erupted following my calls. As unpleasant as this could be, it was still far better than being picked last and then missing the ball. And anyway, first base was under a shady tree.

Well, on one of my recess rendezvous with the encyclopedia, the principal Mr. Guthrie and another teacher saw me studying the diagram of the innards of a camera. Mr. Guthrie asked me if I had ever done any developing. Of course, I hadn't. He said he'd bring in some equipment and show me how it was done. There was a closet under the stairs in the back hall. You could get in if you walked on your knees. We set up a darkroom with his box enlarger, three trays, a safe light and a bucket of water from the well. This started a lifelong hobby.

By this time, I had learned to draw diagrams of pumps and steam engines and car motors. I could sketch out electrical circuits, on the basis that electricity flows from positive to negative, and imagined building all sorts of things. I wondered if I could build a clock that would ring the school bells for the whole day. I drew pictures and decided if the circuit went through both the hour and the minute hands, it would work.

The school bell used to rung by hand, but now an electric bell was installed over the back entrance. This was a large doorbell with wires stapled along the door frame to a button and transformer on the inside of the door. I knew the transformer reduced the voltage to 8 volts, which would not shock you.

I took an old wind-up alarm clock (people gave me things like that) and I cut a copper disk with protrusions at each hour segment where the bell would ring. I glued this to the center of the clock face using cardboard as insulation. I then bent copper strips backed with paper to form clips placed over the edge of the clock face to match the minute intervals for each bell. I cut an hour hand to contact the disk and a minute hand to touch the ring of clips on the outer edge. The clips were tied together as one terminal and the disk was the other.

Mr. Guthrie was sufficiently impressed by the looks of the thing to take the button loose from the door frame and hook it up. It rang at all the right times during the day but was declared a failure (by me) because the minute hand moved so slowly that the duration of each ring was, annoyingly, too long.

There were other good memories of White Hall. In the sixth and seventh grades the teachers organized a kind of soup kitchen. A couple of days a week they cooked soup or rice and raisins on a hot plate in the storage room upstairs. We were asked to bring in canned vegetables for the soup. I don't know who supplied the rice and raisins, but this was the staple. This supplemented our cold lunch box sandwiches brought from home. It was great.

There was the year the school term was extended from eight months to nine months. This decision was made later in the year and we spent much of that extra month on class hikes and reading under the oaks in the school yard.

My favorite teacher at White Hall was Miss Funk. She read *Tom Sawyer* and *Huckleberry Finn* to us in the late evenings if we finished our work in time. She was a good teacher, except for geography, where she made us write out all the answers to all the questions at the end of each chapter. She gave me special privileges to develop pictures, but there was one time when I went too far. When I spent most of a month running bell wire around the building to make an intercom from Mr. Guthrie's room using an old radio he had brought in, she gave me all "I"s on my report card. I didn't understand and neither did my father.

I also remember visits from the county supervisor. On one visit she brought her phonograph and said she had something special she wanted us to hear. She placed the little black box on the teachers desk, opened the lid, placed the crank in the slot and gave it several turns. She then took a shiny record from it's cover and placed it on the turntable. She explained the record was by a famous opera singer named Marian Anderson and that she was singing a song in Latin called *Ave Maria*.

When the steel needle of the reproducer fell into the shellac groove of the 78 record, the sound that came from the folded horn of the cabinet was somewhat less than perfect. Eugene snickered and looked at Jim, covering his mouth with his hand and finally forcing a straight face. I had been conditioned by my brother and the other field hands to think of this kind of sound as "the fat lady screaming". But now, I attempted, truly, to listen. I had not felt the urge to join the initial snicker, but neither did I feel it wise to declare my true feeling just then. I thought it was beautiful.

Many years later, I sat with my college buddies in the front row of the balcony of Richmond's Mosque Theater and heard Marian Anderson in concert. That memory is a clutter of incongruities. To think of me, a hillbilly from Appalachia, sitting with my best friend, a premed whose father was a doctor in Puerto Rico, along with a government major, descended from the blue blood of the Old Dominion, listening to a black woman sing in German on a stage patterned after a

149

Moorish fortress, — all of this in Virginia in 1947 — was at least improbable.

Then, as the final encore, the first clear phrase of the *Ave Maria* rose to fill the intervening space. For me, all else receded into a warm gray haze, and I, of no more substance, hovered there, until the last tone subsided. I had heard Marian Anderson. I had heard something special.

Marian Anderson in 1940 (by Carl Van Vechten)

Stonewall

I came to the new school when it opened in 1941. This was before Jim Hutton had named it Stonewall. Well, not really, but that's the way I thought of it. Jim had always been good at history and wars and things like that. For me, the building was a marvel. Huge, with an auditorium, a stage with foot-lights that folded into the floor, central heating, re-strooms and a science room with a lab table that had a sink with running water. It was all new and shiny and wonderful. But then, to see it this way, perhaps, you had to have been there and to have come from White Hall.

Stonewall High School

From the emotional high of the new building there was also the somber reality of classes starting. I had never been a very good student, that was for Jim and Mary Ellen. I dreaded flash cards, writing out geography questions, and reading aloud. But now, for the first time, it was different. There were so many things to do: gym, typing, science, the school paper, and later, geometry, plain and solid. And now, some of the teachers lectured and you took notes. I felt accepted for what I did well and helped with things I did poorly.

Since Stonewall was the first public high school in our area,[23] some of the teachers understood that some basic training in the social graces was in order.

---

[23] There was an 1869-70 law establishing free public education in Virginia, but, in practice, many Virginia public schools only went up to eighth grade. Wealthier families paid for private high schools.

151

Teachers had student parties in their homes and Miss Jolliffe packed us rough farm kids off to dancing class. *Voilà,* school dances!

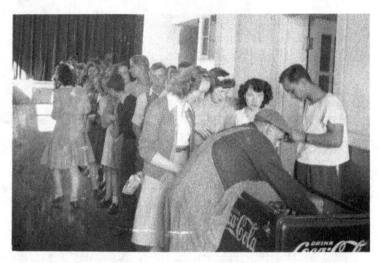

Glen took this at a Stonewall school dance

In athletics, I was never forced to play baseball but was permitted to play soccer and go out for track. I was on the track team and tried to high jump but was never good at it. I liked soccer. We never had a formal team and no one ever knew exactly what the rules were, but it was fun and good exercise.

I never understood why, but for some reason, I was on the football team. I was 6'1" and weighed 130 pounds. Most of my bones were visible from the outside. I was tall enough to be an end but I couldn't catch a pass. They tried me at center; maybe they were thinking of basketball. Here, I couldn't remember the number on which to snap the ball in each play, so they just called "hike" and left me there. Maybe it was because I could, after snapping the ball, do a full length body block. Now in six-man football, with my length, this would take out — or slow down — about half of the line. I got stepped on a lot, but I got a school letter.

Stonewall's football team. Glen is probably taking the picture.

My greatest love, after photography, was the school paper. With all that hi-tech equipment, a mimeograph, a light table, a T-square and, best of all, a typewriter, I couldn't stay away. I could tolerate ink on my hands and could eventually get a readable copy from the mimeograph. I learned to use lettering guides and I did some art work. They once used one of my poems, but now I can't remember the first two lines of the last verse. My greatest accomplishment was devising a simple system to right adjust the two column page. Typewriters didn't do that in those days.

Once we, or I guess, I, had built some overhead lights for the stage, we could close the curtains, and use the space as a newspaper office. With the other demands for the stage, this office came and went. This was very disruptive to a dedicated newspaper man. In my final years I thought I should be editor. My English teacher laughed. So, Publisher was as close as I came. This, I guess, was about right.

I am glad I took Spanish in high school. Being completely inept at language, I spent more time studying Spanish than any other subject in school. I've had no practical use for the language *per se*. However, it was through a foreign language that I began to understand grammar. In about the fifth grade, I remember being told that "am" was part of the verb "to be". I puzzled over that for years. It wasn't until I took Spanish that I understood. I at least learned enough Spanish so that I understood when my band of Spanish friends in college jokingly referred to me as "the great white father."

With the new school, all of the small elementary

schools were closed and the students were brought to Stonewall. Consequently, it was overcrowded from the beginning. The original room on the right of the entrance was split into an office for the principal and a library, with shelves. But as books accumulated, they were kept next door where there was a full-time teacher. The little room with the shelves was used for small classes — far out subjects like trigonometry, solid geometry and second year Spanish.

As the crowding got worse, part of a hallway was boxed off to form a typing room. The south basement, which had been built with only an outside entrance, had two large rooms. They may have originally been intended for a cafeteria, but this space was converted to classrooms and a stairway was cut in the floor of the stage. This was directly under the switch panel for the stage lights. After this, stage lighting was something of an athletic achievement. I always had the fear of losing my footing, tipping over the railing, legs out through the side curtain and then sliding head first down the stairs.

In spite of the quantum leap of the new building, apparently the planners had come from an era when on one could imagine a student taking a bath at school. There were no showers for athletics. This was a problem for all sports but when football came along, it was impossible.

I don't know how Mr. Harper did it but he managed to solve the problem. A water heater was placed in the coal bin, a line of shower heads strung along a wall in the furnace room, a sump pump in a pit in the floor, a plastic pipe to the gutter by the driveway, and we had showers.

Glen at Stonewall

I can't say I had any one favorite teacher at Stonewall. Miss Jolliffee must have been the best. She lectured, which was the best method for me to get through English, History, and Civics. And then there was a 'worst' teacher. He sold insurance and tried to teach Algebra. I can't remember his name, but oddly enough, Algebra has been the one high school subject that I've used the most through the years in all of my work with computers, writing complex FORTRAN programs.

I always thought Stonewall was a warm and friendly place. It wasn't until I was there one weekend working alone that I realized it wasn't the place but the people that created this warmth.

Without my asking, Mr. Harper, the principal,

found me summer jobs working for the government, which paid much better than any other local work. In fact, it paid well enough to cover half of my room and board through college. He also arranged a working tuition scholarship for me to the University of Richmond. I never understood exactly how this was done. It was somehow through the Baptist Church in Winchester. This was something of a stretch for a Methodist who privately believed that science, including evolution, was just man's attempt to understand and truly appreciate God's creation.

Years later, when I tried to teach at James Wood School, I came to understand what a unique experience Stonewall had been. I now see this was due to the attitude brought to Stonewall by Mr. Harper and his teachers. There was trust and respect and the freedom that follows from these.

As a student, I felt I was part of the school, part of the system. There was no reason for us-against-them schemes to fool or outmaneuver the system. There were no hall passes. Before and after classes, all that waiting-for-the-bus time, we were free to study, mingle, visit, socialize — to be young people. It was a given that we knew how to behave. Only if actions were unacceptable were there rules and punishment. Your word was respected and its value guarded. I believe it is only through this clear expression of trust

157

and respect that a student can understand the obliga-
tion and value of personal integrity.

And Then I Went Off To College

by Glen Whitacre

Prologue

"And then I went off to college..." might be a throwaway line in someone else's story, but college was not inevitable for the son of an orchardman. Given that, I'm surprised how little I can remember about the initial phase of this endeavor. I'm sure I always thought I'd go to college. My brother George went, but I can't remember ordering college catalogs or reading them in a library or even thinking of one school instead of another. I can't even remember ever worrying about how it would be paid for.

My brother had played football and had an on-campus job but he had to beg money from my father and there never seemed to be any understanding of how much he needed or how much my father would pay. But then my brother had a car and car expenses in high school. We had such little in common. We were eight years apart. He was the raging bull. I was the sickly kid. So I never thought of him as a model for going to college, good or bad.

As I look back now, money should have been the primary concern. My father had managed an orchard which was owned by an insurance salesman and the proprietor of a clothing store. His highest cash salary was $42.50 per month. This was not a living wage even in 1938. So, as part of the job he was provided with a house, ground for gardens, and space to raise chickens (for eggs and meat), cows (for milk), and hogs (for meat).

Nearly all of the gardening was done by my mother and us kids. The initial plowing and harrowing were done by my father using the company's mules. The planting, cultivating, weeding, and gathering were left to us with the possible exception of plowing out potatoes in the fall which would be done by my father with the mule's help.

There was no freezer (no electricity) so the food that fed the family was all prepared and canned by my mother with some help from any kids not in school or working for a salary. The cows were milked and fed and the stalls cleaned before and after the ten hour work day. Chickens provided us with meat and eggs. Sometimes we had extra eggs to sell, which helped pay for groceries we needed to buy at the store. The

160

family's only other meat came from the hogs. We fed them from table scraps and added a little corn to their diet in the fall. Once the hogs were big and the weather was cold, butchering day was a family and community exchange effort. The meat was canned and cured to last through the year by my mother and father.

My mother collected the cream from the two or three gallons of milk she got from the cows each day. She also sold cream to help buy groceries (sugar, salt, flour, etc.) from the store. As I remember, the cream would bring about $2.00 a week.

The orchard had one other full-time tenant who lived in a house there and worked full time. There was enough work to keep him and my father busy through-out the winter. He was paid $30.00 per month and received similar privileges. He could keep a cow, if he had one, and pigs, chickens and a garden. During the months of September and October there were 20 to 30 employed during the picking and packing of the fall apples.

My brother, after he was fifteen of so, worked full time in summer for 12 1/2 cents an hour, which was the adult daily wage. I started at twelve working at intermittent jobs like replanting corn, making hay or picking early apples at 10 cents an hour.

I think of Jimps' Orchard as "where I grew up." We moved into the tenant house when I was about six, my father's boss drank too much and was fired the next year. We moved into the bigger house when my father was made manager. My father stayed there for nine and a half years. This was unusual as he had moved after one year from his two previous jobs. I, of course, didn't know why he left these jobs, it could have been because he asked for a raise or it could have been that he didn't like the people or the place.

Jimps' Orchard

Leaving his first orchard job must have been a terrific blow. It was an orchard owned by a lawyer and I get the impression that it was owned almost as a hobby and certainly as a mountain retreat. My father was in his thirties, and the lawyer set up fishing trips and overnight hunting parties with my father, brother, uncles and cousins.

The hillbilly sport of hunting was first for food and pelts to sell but it was also a social thing of group camaraderie and friendship. The lawyer loved my mother's cooking and was treated as one of the family. He gave my father a walnut desk and a leather chair. I was named after his son. These must have been the best of times for my father.

But my brother got into some serious legal trouble. He took his hunting rifle to school. As I remember it, he used the gun to shoot off the telephone insulators along the road as target practice and then left a few bullet holes in the school house door for effect. No one was hurt, and I don't know if anyone was really threatened, but it was serious enough that he was sent off to live with our grandfather, in another state, for the rest of the year.

No one has ever told me why he did this, but from an off hand comment George made to me many years later, I suspect my father tried to publicly embarrass him about wetting the bed. The men at the country store, — the only community hang out — had overheard. Well, for this, or some other reason, my father left this job and found another job in another state.

So it had been a very stable nine and one half years for me as I grew up, but the last three years of high school were very different. Abruptly, after my freshman year, in the middle of summer, my father quit his job and we moved. I don't know the whole story but it involved a newly hired tenant hand who was not following my father's work instructions. Then one day the owner came and went directly into the orchard to talk to the tenant. My mother saw this happening and went to the barn where she overheard some of the conversation. Apparently the owner had offered to deal separately with the tenant.

The mode of operation had always been that my father would visit the owner's office on Saturday afternoon every week or so, and after a report of the current status, would be given general instructions. The day-to-day operations were left to my father. The owner visited the orchard only occasionally just to look around and talk to my father.

My father knew that this new arrangement could not work and so he quit. We concluded that the owner knew my father would quit and it was, thus, intentional. As to why, I don't know. My father was a hard worker and a tough task master for us and the other workers. He enforced a fifty-five hour week. He chose the easier, standing rider position on the spray rig, but he was the boss. In the off-season, if he had a chore in town, he might make half a day of it. He had a gas pump installed for the machinery and had permission to use this gas in his own car. He had built a cistern in the basement and my mother now had a water pump and sink in the kitchen. So, over his nine years working at Jimps, my father had developed a few perks.

The owner may also been concerned that my brother was about to graduate from college and would likely leave the orchard and that I wouldn't be far behind. The other tenant worker had several children, who would probably not finish grade school, and could thus provide the cheapest of labor force for some time to come.

My father had always been very secretive about his finances. Somehow, over his now fifty years, he had accumulated enough to buy a small farm about five miles away. It was something over forty acres and, in this deepest of the Depression, I think he paid $3500 or $3900, or something like that. It had been the main house of a much larger farm, which we found out later went back to the 1840's. The family had fallen on hard times and had sold off the frontage along the roads on two sides, leaving only about 40 acres. Since the house was built before there were roads, it was now on the far corner, away from both roads, and there were long muddy lanes leading in from each.

The house had been quite grand in its time. Its time, of course, did not include electricity, plumbing or central heat. It was brick and L-shaped. The main leg had four large rooms, each with a fireplace ,and there was a large central hall with stairs, open from the first floor into the attic. The small leg was a large kitchen room with a walk-in fireplace at the end and a separate stairway to the three-quarter loft over the kitchen. We presumed this had been for servants at some time.

Ridgeway, near Inwood, West Virginia, after it had been painted yellow. It is now registered as an historic house: The James Nathanial Burwell House. At some point, a kitchen was added to the back, making the house a L shaped.

The owners had long since abandoned this house, had moved to the city, and had rented it to ten-ants. It had now reached a state of decay with hanging strips of wallpaper and kid's graffiti on the plaster

166

walls. The back porch was rotting and the wooden steps had collapsed.

On closer inspection of the basement, the house once had central heating, A coal furnace had been added sometime after 1863, which was patent date on the exterior of the furnace. It was a large octopus of a thing, with pipes flaring up through the floors and the chimney. The pipes had long since rusted through and most had been carted away. The ash pit of the furnace had now sunk into the clay and the outer shell was rusted thin and was loose to the touch. This later installation of the furnace had closed off all of the fire places and two of them were irreparably altered.

Well, in the middle of summer, without any time for renovation, we moved into this house. The time of year was an embarrassment to my father; orchardmen moved in March which was the lull in the crops.

The house itself, even in this condition, was not that much of a shock. In fact it was typical of any move from one orchard to another. The house we were moving from had one similar design feature. It, too, had a large central hall going up to the attic and had once been the big house. There had been the remains of slave quarters when we first moved there. My father had taken them apart and used the logs to build new hog pens.

But this was our house, now my house, and I

could see it for what it had been and what I wanted it to be. My father had applied for power to be run in under the Rural Electrification Act[24]. This had been done by the power company without any further input from us and this turned out to be the first wart on my vision. In this open country, with the house looking out on the farm, there was now a pole in the front yard with a transformer hanging on it and wires running in to the front porch with a meter box by the front door. It was ugly. I blew up. The transformer should have been near the barn and the wires brought in to the end of the house. Finally, my father agreed to see if the power company would change it. They removed the pole from the front yard, moved the transformer back to the next pole up the line and placed a shorter pole between the house and the barn to direct the wires to the end of the house.

I'm not sure of the timing of all of this but Dad did whatever was needed in the barn and chicken house to take care of the animals we had brought with us. He repaired the back porch floor and I helped him drag in some concrete pillars to form steps.

There were two serious structural problems with the house. The outer walls were solid three bricks thick and rested on a foundation of field stone which

---

[24] The Rural Electrification Act of 1936 provided federal loans for the installation of distribution in rural areas.

was also the outside wall of the basement. This had been laid with soft homemade mortar and, when the furnace was installed, a hole had been knocked through the stone to install a coal shoot. This had caused the wall at the end of the house to crack and there was now a two inch gap along the window frame on that corner. This had also twisted the cupboards in the dining room so that the doors would not close.

One of the two interior walls in the main part of the house was also solid brick and extended down to the floor of the basement. The bricks were soft, probably "burned" on the farm, and had begun to disintegrate in the damp basement. This had pulled the two door openings in that wall out of square by more than an inch.

My father refilled the coal shoot hole with stone and mortar. I fitted pieces of brick along the window frame to match the original as best I could. I also took the cupboard frames loose from the wall in the dining room and replaced them square enough for the doors to close. We tried jacking up the wall to straighten the doorways but didn't have a jack that was large enough. We did build a form around the wall in the basement and fill it with concrete to stop the disintegration.

As was the custom, my sister Velma came to help for several days. After we scrubbed and cleaned every inch of the house, we treated the bedrooms for bed bugs. Then I helped my sister wallpaper several of the rooms. The woodwork was scarred with splits and pieces missing. Even when it was clean, it was still a dirty brown. In my vision it had to be white — all white — like the movies. I set about to repair and paint. Work on the central hall with the three story stairway to the attic took two years.

My pride and joy was restoring the original box locks on the living room and the two outside doors from the hall. I cleaned and polished the brass, cleaned the steel metal parts and painted them black. The final step was to make a key that would operate the lock on the front door.

In the next year my father acquired two mules and bought an old Fordson tractor. This was the original 1927 version, with steel wheels, similar to the one we had had on the orchard. For an old tractor, it was in good condition. It would start — and that tended to be a problem for that model. Then with some advice from Uncle Tull, who had done the same with his Fordson, I installed a down draft carburetor to replace the evaporative unit which was designed to burn kerosene. For the carburetor I had chosen, I had to redesign the check valve because of the low head of the gas tank but then it worked very well.

The next year my father found a double plow that would bolt onto the tractor. It had no wheels but was lifted directly by a lever. There were no hydraulics. There was some counter balance from a spring but using it was very hard physical work. I have that plow to thank for the development of some pecs on my skin-and-bones body.

Plowing with this thing in the blue limestone fields of the Shenandoah Valley was not only hard work but tedious. At one point my father thought I was working too slowly and he took over to show me how it should be done. In one trip around the field he had broken three plow points. He gave it back to me and didn't complain any more.

This was all in the background of World War II. As I approached draft age, my father thought I stood a better chance of getting a farm deferment if we were working on a larger farm. He found a farm that would take us as share croppers and we moved there. This was owned by a doctor who had bought the farm from a spinster with the understanding he would provide a home for her for the rest of her life. He had built himself a small house but as she became more feeble, he had moved his family into the big house with her. The little house was the nicest house we had ever lived in.

Meanwhile my brother had been drafted and his wife and two daughters came to live with us. When my call did come it was during the bad days of the Battle of the Bulge. When I went for my physical, it was discovered that my right arm had been broken as a young child and the bones had healed crooked so that my arm didn't work properly. I had only 40% of nor-

George was drafted in WWII

mal rotation of my right hand. Then when it was found that I had calcification on my lungs from previous infections, I was given a 4F classification.[25]

We continued working on the farm until the war ended. After we moved, I had dropped out of school in the middle of my senior year. After the war was over I went back to school and we moved back to the family farm. In reality, this was only a subsistence opera-

tion. We could raise enough food to feed ourselves and the animals through the winter but there was no cash money income. My father wanted to look for another share cropping situation. I did not.

Finally he has able to get a job driving a school bus. This would mesh nicely with the farm work but it was a nine month job and the salary was $100 per

---

[25] Glen told family members the calcifications were from a lung infection he caught from the chicken coup (histoplasmosis). He also had double pneumonia as a child, which can cause calcification.

month.   This was more cash income than he had earned before but hardly adequate to hobnob with ideas of college.

Then one day in that last half of my senior year, Mr. Harper, the school principal, called me into his office.   He said he wanted me to meet Dr. Clark, the minister of the First Baptist Church in Winchester. He said he thought Dr. Clark might be able to get me some help with tuition at Richmond College which was part of the University of Richmond.

Mr. Harper arranged a time and took me to meet Dr. Clark. I felt completely out of place and thought I had left no winning impression, but Mr. Harper's recommendations must have gone a long way.   A few days later I was informed I had been granted a working scholarship for my full tuition.

We got verification of this from Richmond.   It also came with what I thought was very bad news. Due to the increased enrollment of the veterans now attending under the GI Bill, there would be no campus housing for freshman and I was advised that I should make my own arrangements.   For a naive farm kid who thought of the city of Richmond as a far off and exotic place that I had only seen burn in *Gone With The Wind* and whose overall experience in any city was limited to family trips to the zoo in Washington, DC, this was a major problem.

Then Mrs. Kersey, my Spanish teacher, came to my rescue. She had lived in Richmond for some years when her husband had been a minister there. She said she still had friends there and she was sure someone could find me a place to stay. Sometime later she brought me a postcard which said there was a Johnson family who lived in walking distance to the college. She said they were already taking two students and she was sure they could take another. She said the Johnsons were an elderly couple, retired, and a good Christian family and that the other students were studying for the ministry. She suggested we contact the Johnsons right away. There was an address and when I asked Mrs. Kersey if she could tell me how to find it, she volunteered to go with me to Richmond.

As I said, I'm not sure of the time sequence here, but in that same half year, Mr. Harper said he thought he may have a job for me to earn some extra money. Well, I thought the word "extra" was inappropriate, but I said, "Sure, how's that?"

He went on to explain that he, Neil and Bobby had been working for the Bureau of Entomology for the past two summers. They operated quarantine stations along US 11 to control the migration of Japanese beetle on produce trucks. He said they operated from June to September and that it was a good summer job. Of course I was interested. He said he would recommend me for the job and that a Mr. Kelly, from Philadelphia, would be contacting me in early June. This was unexpected and great. Now I would have money for room and board. It didn't occur to me until I'm writing this that Mr. Harper didn't work that next year. Was it his job I had taken?

On the day appointed by Mrs. Kersey, she, my mother and I set off for Richmond. It was indeed a long way. Down the Shenandoah Valley, over the mountains to Fredericksburg and then south on US 1, the largest and busiest highway I had ever driven on, and into the northern edge of the city. There were block after block of large brick houses, all under trees, and they went on and on for miles. So much alike. How could you find your way?

Then Mrs. Kersey pointed out that we were approaching Broad Street. She said it was the principle thoroughfare and that the Capitol and large department stores were to the east but that we should turn west toward Westhampton. This was indeed a broad street. Its double east and west lanes were separated by a median with double trolley tracks. There were electric trolleys speeding along with the cars.

After a few miles west we turned off of Broad Street into a grid of more brick houses and trees. These were grander as we went along block after block. After several miles, the orderly array of streets became a maze of intersections and Mrs. Kersey said we were approaching the campus. Mrs. Kersey directed the turns and there on our right was the address.

It was a large, square, formal, brick house with white trim and a slate roof. Mrs. Johnson met us at the door and invited us into the living room. She was very cordial, and the house — this was class all the way. I wondered if I could maintain this degree of polish. She said she already had four students in the two rooms on the third floor but she was converting a small room on the main floor and thought she would have room for me if I liked the room. She then proceeded to show us the room, which, to my surprise, was off the living room through double French doors. The room was what I would call a sun porch except it was on the north side. It had full windows along the end and the back and looked out from a second story onto the back yard which receded below to a small stream. The reddish brown trunks of the ancient pines went up close to the windows and flared out into a green canopy high above the house. It was great.

There was a sofa and a desk in the room. She said the sofa would fold down into a bed and she would bring down a chest of drawers for my clothes. There was another door to a hallway leading to the kitchen. She pointed out that there was a powder room there off the hall which I could use and that there was a full bath on the second floor which I could share with the other boys. Except for the close proximity to the kitchen and the living room, the whole thing seemed excellent to me.

She said we could keep things in the refrigerator if we labeled them and the boys were welcome to join her husband and herself in the living room in the evenings. She said, "On cold nights we usually have a fire in the fire place."

I don't remember the price but we accepted and agreed on the date I would move in before freshman orientation. We said our goodbyes and struck off to see the campus.

The street curved off to the left among the mix of houses, mostly similar materials and under the old pines, but each individual in design. There was grass, flowers, and late, mature shrubs, a little overgrown but natural and neat.

As the road swung back to the right the houses ended and there were large buildings off in the distance through the trees. Mrs. Kersey explained that the men's college was there on the right and that the women's college was to the left on the other side of the lake. For an instant, the word "moat" came to mind, but it was a beautiful little lake between three hills. None of the Westhampton (women's) buildings were visible except the chapel's rose window which could be seen through the trees. All else was obscured by the thick forest covering the hillside rising from the lake.

On the men's side there were two hills. The first was topped by what seemed to be a cathedral-sized library. Between it and the towers of the administration building ran an open covered walk with doors to class-rooms along the wall. Halfway down the hill to the east was a flat quadrangle with the science building forming the three sides. On the other hill were two strung out dormitories fitted into the hill among the trees. Further on there was the gymnasium, set back on the crest of the hill and a large building with a sign "Refectory". This, I learned later, was the dining hall.

It was all ivy-covered brick and stone with arches, towers, dormers and leaded windows. There were a few panels of oak frame and waddle. It was Shakespeare. It was English movies. It was great.

We located the parking area for the admin-istration building and I went in to ask about the schol-arship. The clerk or secretary spent a few seconds at a file and came back.

"Is that Charles Glenvil, Mr. Whitacre?" She paused a little with my spelling of Glenvil. The "Mr." was an elevation of status that I hadn't expected. I stammered a little before I answered.

"Yes, ma'am, that's right."

"Your tuition will be fully covered. That is $75

University of Richmond's "cathedral sized"
Boatwright Memorial Library

per semester. We ask you to work eight hours a week. You can work that out according to your class schedule."

"Do you know what I'll be doing?"

"Well, no. It will depend on your schedule. It will probably be here in the administration building. Come back and see Dean Gray after you have your schedule. He will tell you all about it then."

There was a warm friendly attitude of helpfulness. As I went back to the car, I repeated "and see Dean Gray". This is real livin'.

In early June a government car came to the farm. There were forms to be filled out and Mr. Kelly told me I would be hired as a GS-4, Inspector at a salary of $1902 *per annum*. That was, or course, minus taxes but he said I'd get that back at the end of the year. I wasn't going to work an *annum*, but this was more money than I could imagine.

He explained what I would have to buy the uniform. Then, he added, since I was the new addition to the crew, it was the custom that I would get the night shift from midnight to 8 a.m. That is unless one of the other fellows would like that shift. If not, I was stuck with it. But there was one more unkind cut, the night man filled and cleaned the lanterns and smudge pots. This was a carbon black, dirty job.

The work schedule violated all the rules of nature and farming. I couldn't fall asleep at 9 a,m, on a summer's day. I would wander off to work on the farm or the house. Inevitably, it wouldn't go as I expected and I'd still be working in mid-afternoon, or later, before I forced myself to go to bed. My father didn't ask me to do extra work on the farm, but I always felt he expected me to help with critical jobs like making hay.

With all of this diversity the summer went by rapidly. I had accumulated more than $200. We got the packet of literature from Richmond College which spelled out the schedule for freshman orientation and gave semester prices for three meals a day at the refectory. I could buy a meal ticket and have some left over for rent.

Freshman Year

Now the actual going off to college could be written up as a comedy with overtones of the *Beverly Hillbillies*, but I didn't see it that way. For me it was deadly serious. I don't remember how many went on the journey, but it was a family affair. I think it was my brother, mother, father and I but my sister-in-law Virginia may have come along, also. The usual mode would have been to take a picnic lunch and eat in the park even if it meant eating out of the trunk of the car. I know we did that on other visits of the family.

Glen at University of Richmond

Since this was a long trip and was looked on as a moving, I suspect we arrived in the early afternoon. After Mr. and Mrs. Johnson greeted everyone, we carried my clothes and a few boxes of my belongings into the room, and then I directed them on a drive around the campus. We then went back to the house and said goodbye in all possible pair and group combinations, but no one turned to leave. Several times someone commented that it was late, and it was a long trip. Finally, they assembled in the car and backed out of the driveway. Everybody waved, and I stood in the yard waving back. They were gone.

Mrs. Johnson had told my mother that she would leave something in the kitchen for the boys because she knew the dining hall wasn't open yet. I can't remember what I ate or if I ate, I just remember being cold in that room alone, both physically and spiritually. I had never been lonely when I was alone, only when I had nothing that interested me, nothing to do. Having left everything mechanical and academic behind, I had nothing to do. I was lonely. It was a long evening. The fold down sofa was hard and it was a long time before I fell asleep.

When my alarm went off the next morning, I washed up, shaved, brushed my hair and left with an adrenaline high to the unknown. The dining hall was the first challenge. Eating in public, except for sandwiches at school, was new. The mass cooked food, scrambled eggs on the verge of green, a tangled mass of bacon, precooked pancakes aligned in a tray, white mush like grits, dry cereal in little boxes, a carton of milk and a cup of coffee, all to be passed over or taken in the indentations of a metal tray in the hustle of a moving line. It was hectic. The tables were large, maybe three-by-eight feet so you found a seat and nodded to the people across from you. They all seemed to know each other and were engaged in noisy interchanges. There must have been other freshman, so there must have been other lost souls like myself, but I didn't see any.

The orientation sessions went on schedule. Among the many things we were told, there was one that was very good news. Due to the great increase in enrollment, the usual razzing of Freshmen would be limited to wearing the beanie and carrying the orientation booklet. Further, this was just to identify us as new on campus so that we could get help if we needed it. (Now that was a switch.) We welcomed the change, but most of us were smart enough to realize that the older returning veterans were not about to be pushed around by the, probably younger, upperclassmen. It was a practical choice.

The beanies thinned and disappeared altogether within a few days. At first, the beanies made me feel part of the group, part of the gang. But once I inspected my image in a mirror, realized it made me look about ten-years-old. So, my freshman beanie went to the back of a drawer.

On one of those first days, before I knew

anyone well enough to ask them to come along, I walked to the campus trolley stop and waited for a car to arrive. When the door folded open and the conductor stared down at me my body knew what a new and novel adventure this was. I made it up the steps without tripping and attempted to hand the fare to the conductor. He said, "Put it in the box," like he had to tell all the yokels that.

The box looked something like a pay telephone except the top section was glass on all four sides and the top was an open funnel. When the coin, a dime, was dropped in the top it went down a little shoot, reversed direction, and stopped on the slant of the floor of the glass compartment facing the conductor. He then pushed a lever and it disappeared into the larger bottom of the box. This seemed a lot of action to collect a dime. I found out later that the lower part of the box sorted the coins also.

No one else had gotten on at the campus trolley stop. I took a seat and slid over to the window looking at the shrubs and tree limbs flash by as we wormed around the hill from the campus. The trolley turned onto the median of the thoroughfare, past the village and down the straight-of-way through the blocks of brick houses.

Now that I was on my way, maybe it was the adrenalin kickback, but there was a sense of freedom I don't think I had felt before. Maybe for some it was like when a kid first gets his drivers license. But not for me, there were strings attached there. Now, it was like there were no strings attached. I didn't have to tell anybody where I was going, or why I was going, or when I'd be back. I could make up the day as I went along and not have to explain to anybody when I came back. It was new. It was great.

We stopped whenever there were people standing on the platform near the track. They dropped their coins in the box and sat down. I wondered how you told the driver where you wanted to get off. There was a cord along the top of the windows. Was that it, or was that the emergency cord like I'd seen on the train in the movies?

We turned across several blocks and then onto Broad Street. Now I was coming to the stores and I had to know how to get off. Finally, there was the ding, ding of a bell. There was a hand on the cord above the windows, the trolley began to slow down and stopped at the next platform. O.K.!

Hey, there's a theater. I pulled the cord and walked to the front. As the trolley slowed down, I asked, "What trolley do I take to go back to school?"

"Any Westhampton."

I got off and walked back to the theater. I went up to the ticket booth and placed the money on the sill and slid it in through the opening, "One."

I looked at the girl, she hadn't pushed the key to eject the ticket. She was black and young. She seemed unsure of what to say, "Your theater is farther down the street."

"My theater?"

"Sir, this is a colored theater."

"Oh." I turned in the direction she had pointed. I didn't know there were colored theaters. Then I got to thinking, I'd never seen a black in the theaters at home. It wasn't until I inquired later that I found out that those theaters had a special section of the balcony and a separate stairway. I hadn't thought of it before.

Between the orientation sessions, there were a few who had not already intertwined with fraternity or other connections and we wondered around inspecting each other's name tags and making offhand small talk hoping to strike up a conversation. In one of these interchanges, a kid, who looked even younger than I felt, introduced me to another, even younger looking still. He said his name was Api and he was from Puerto Rico. This was like a flare.

In high school I had become obsessed with Spanish. I could construct no logical reason or defense for this. I had no facility with language, Spanish or English, and the time I had spent drilling myself was unreasonable. I could recite all 180 endings for the regular verbs and knew most of the irregular verbs. I knew the alphabet, in Spanish, the whole number system, the days of the week, the months, much more than any American student of a foreign language should know. I didn't understand this, either. Was it the mystery? Was it memory from a former life? Still, I was an addict, even if I couldn't remember enough vocabulary to say anything useful. But in West Virginia in 1946, I had never met anyone who actually spoke Spanish. I could not pass up this opportunity.

I soon found that Api's complete name was Rafael Angel Munoz Noya. His father was a doctor in Puerto Rico and he was in the premed program and planned to become a doctor himself. He had studied English in school but had had little practice in speaking it. He was fifteen but looked much younger and his interest and confusion in this strange gringo world was too great an opportunity for me to miss.

Then there was registration day. It seemed each professor had his own booth or something. I didn't understand it then, and I don't understand it now. There were long lines, slow lines and it took all day. So now I had my schedule, it was time to go see Dean Gray about my campus job assignment. I don't think Dean Gray was available. I was told to come back after the confusion was over.

In the days that followed I sought out opportunities to continue these conversations with Api. His home was in a small town called Manati. He referred to servants and thus a world I couldn't imagine but I wanted to learn. Yes, he had a girl in Puerto Rico but as he continued to explain, she was much more than "a girl". The two families had already agreed that they would become engaged. No, the parents had not made the choice. They had met while properly chaperoned and had fallen in love. There had been one occasion when they had eluded their chaperone at the beach. This was a matter of great concern and gravity to both families. It was not proper behavior for an *hombre sensato*, a young man of good intentions. This did not show proper respect for her or her family. But now it had all been arranged — he would marry Armina when he graduated.

The reverse flow, in this interchange, were some details of my own family. Perhaps I colored it a little, making it a little more what I thought it should be, but I didn't lie.

I tried to help with phrases and idioms. Api spoke with the typical accent that we consider charming and he had no intention in losing it, but some words just didn't come out acceptably. The most troublesome was "sheet". As he said it, it was a familiar four letter word. We practiced on and on, "she" and "eat". He could say these separately, but putting them together came out "she" "it"

I went to Mass once with Api. I was confused
and amazed by the ritual. After the long incantation in
Latin (with elaborate back-up in costume), the priest
came sweeping down the aisle. His robes caught in the
breeze as he was flinging holy water left and right and
trailing a fog of incense like a vapor trail. It was a
spectacle, the finale, I thought, and I watched with
fixed attention. As the Priest swept by, my stare was
met by his disapproving glare. This seemed very un-
friendly. Then I realized I was supposed to be bowed
for his blessing.

This was how I felt, but I would never have
talked to Api in this vein. He attended the required
chapel at school and we often attended the First Baptist Church downtown. As a spectator, though, I was
fascinated by the Catholic Church. It seemed the key.
It was either the remnant of the Spanish culture or the
basis of the Spanish culture. I tried to imagine church
school, being drilled in one ritual of belief. But I
would not criticize his belief, I knew I could hold my
own.

This was a new and fascinating world. In
private times I tried to imagine it in more detail. I
wondered if this constant policing by the chaperone
system is in itself a clear statement that any girl and
boy left alone would immediately have sexual inter-

course. Would this be so ingrained in the psyche that anything less would be considered unnatural, and for the boy, unmanly? Of course, I didn't discuss this, either, at this level. The locker room syndrome prevails; this maintains the proper distance to keep your options open.

I did try to advise him on what to expect, but from my limited experience, this wasn't much: Her parents expect to know something about the boy. At least that's what the girl will tell them. Well, yes, at some social levels her family will have to know his family, but I wouldn't know about that. They'll want to know where you're going, who will be there and they'll tell you what time she must be home. They expect the kids to be truthful about all of this. (Don't forget this was the 40's.) What you do on the date, or what you really do, is pretty much up to the girl. It's her responsibility and she'll say "no". I knew it was the guy's responsibility to say "no", too, but I knew he'd never buy that.

Over the next several days, I found that Api had a room in the dorm. Being a "foreign" student he'd been given special consideration. And what a room! It was at the top of the tower in Jeter Hall with windows on two sides looking down on the campus. His roommate was a Junior, and pleasant enough guy, but seemed to have no interest in Spanish culture. After a while he kidded me about these drawn out sessions with Api. I would drift into Api's accent after a while. I'm inclined to do that with any accent but it must have been kind of funny to listen to us. I did want, so desperately, to understand and speak Spanish, but Api had no patience with my feeble attempts, so we spoke English with a Spanish accent.

The session with Dean Gray did occur and I was told my regular job would be to record the chapel attendance. He referred me to one of the secretaries, by name, and said she would explain all of the details. I was told pledge slips were handed out at each chapel session. One was signed by each student and they were collected on the way out. It was my job to record these in a log to check the required attendance. In the previous year dates had been entered on a line for each name on the school roster. It was agreed I would work Tuesday and Thursday afternoons.

When the next Tuesday rolled around, at the appointed time, I reported to the administration office where I was shown the file with the log book and the scramble of pink slips collected that week. The roster from the previous year had been much shorter than the new one. The task was complicated by a different schedule for each class identity. I worked out a matrix of cells in the log book with the nonattendance dates x'ed out for each student. The problem was the signatures. After the nearly legible slips had been ordered alphabetically, the remaining third had to be compared name by name for a "most likely".

"Why can't they print?"

It was explained, "The attendance slip is a legal statement; it requires a signature."

Before the end of the first semester I had gotten up enough nerve to go to the Dean and propose that a line be added to the top with the instruction, "Please print."

He looked hard at my diagram and then said to me. "Would you object to writing your name twice?"

I could only guess he was not expecting an unbiased opinion and I answered, "No sir, I would not."

"Very well, we will have them changed in the next printing."

I thanked him and went off to enjoy my victory. This was short lived. The slips had already been printed for the next semester. They were kept in a vault, I guess, so I didn't know.

My off-campus "sun room facing north" was very nice but always seemed a little cold and lonely. It wasn't comfortable to study in pajamas. I had to wear a robe. This was a novelty, but I did have a robe. I had been advised, by those who would know, that a robe was standard equipment for a college student.

I was struggling with English composition and second-year Spanish, spending hours with both dictionaries, but was just squeezing through the English class because of my spelling. Dr. Ball reduced a grade one letter for each misspelled word.

The powder room just outside the door worked fine. I could shave, brush my teeth, wash my face, etc. there and since I took gym three times a week and always showered there I almost never used the bath on the second floor. After some time, Mrs. Johnson must have noticed this because she very tactfully and rather hesitantly asked if I understood I was welcome to use the bath on the second floor. I was too naive to take this as any kind of criticism but explained that I showered at the school gym. What I didn't say was that three baths a week was more than I had been accustomed to. She withdrew just saying she wanted to be sure I understood.

The Johnsons were perfect landlords. They were quiet in the evenings, they never intruded but would remind us that we were welcome in the living room. I never took them up on that except on my birthday. My mother had sent me a cake. I asked if I could invite the other boys down for cake. She agreed and made a little party of it with drinks and other snacks. The cake had come in the mail; it was somewhat battered but had held together. It was chocolate with bits of walnut and a thick white icing with walnut halves on the surface. Mrs. Johnson took over serving the cake with great praise of my mother's baking. Well, my mother was a good country cook but I knew she hadn't made this cake. Her cakes just weren't that good. But I just smiled and didn't explain my thoughts. Then, with the triangular serving knife, she lifted out the first slice and there at the bottom was the round cardboard disc of a store bought cake. I didn't know how to recover from my fake acceptance of this praise and in my shock, Mrs. Johnson continued serving the cake as if she hadn't noticed.

I did visit the four guys on the third floor occasionally, but we had very little in common. Woodfin, though, was a musician. He played saxophone with dance bands some nights and weekends. This fascinated me. He had his clothes re-tailored after he bought them. I knew he saw me as a novelty — a country bumpkin — but he was never cruel about it. He seemed, honestly, to enjoy my language and points of view. His comments were, essentially, a chuckle.

There was one time when the Johnsons went away for a few days and left us with a list of numbers to call if this or that happened. Well, we didn't have the usual beer party that gets out of hand, which seem mandatory in today's films, but the house did catch fire. Well, not really. One evening someone smelled smoke. We opened the door to the basement from the kitchen and was met by a cloud of smoke collected in the stairwell. Someone ran to the number list and called the fire department. A couple of us went down through the smoke into the basement. I could see the fire was around the furnace which was set in a pit about a foot below the basement floor. Fuel oil had leaked out of the furnace and was on fire in the pit. There was sand or ashes or something there and we started throwing these on the flames. This worked and we had the fire out in a few seconds. We turned off the furnace and when we were sure the fire was all out, I went back upstairs to hear the fire truck coming, roar by and disappear down the street. It did come back. We explained the situation, a couple of firemen inspected the basement, said it looked OK but that we should call the furnace repairman tomorrow.

After some trial and error, I found a path between the backyards over the stream and through the woods to the campus. It was still about half a mile, too far to walk for one period breaks. I had never been able to study in a library. It was too formal, too quiet, too occupied for me to concentrate. I must have commented on this because Api invited me to study in his room if I wanted. This was a godsend for the period between Gym and lunch. Both Api and his roommate had classes this period, so the tower room was all mine for the hour to survey my domain below. I loved it.

By this time, we knew there were two other Spanish speaking students, George (pronounced Horhe) and Carlos. We often met for meals and congregated in a clump along the large community tables in the refectory. They spoke only Spanish among themselves. I didn't know until years later this was an agreed upon commitment they had made to each other. Mostly I didn't understand what was being said. I never thought of this as impolite. One would explain whenever I asked, but mostly I didn't, getting only bits and pieces. I think I told myself I would get it if I kept trying. I never did.

In spite of the signature problem, I managed to keep up with the chapel attendance slips. I think the secretary there liked me. It was something between mother and aunt. One day she came over while I was working and said she was going through my file and noticed what she thought must be a mistake. "It says your father's income is only $900 a year. Is that right?"

Again, I was not embarrassed by this. I explained, "We have our own farm and raise our own food, but the only real cash income he has is from driving the school bus. That is $900."

She listened attentively and looked sympathetic. My inside feeling was, "And look at how well I'm doing." She didn't comment further.

Bobby Crumb, whom we had met on those early confusing days, continued to stop by Api's room. Bobby was a local, maybe fifty miles south of Richmond. I had fun picking up the Richmond accent from him. Stretch the vowels, smooth out the consonants and lose the "r's" when they're hanging on the end like that. It was kind of like novocaine in the tongue. He lived off campus in the opposite direction from me. At one point he invited Api and me home for a weekend. There was some local event, with a dance. It was all arranged — dates and corsages — all very proper. We went.

His father and mother picked us up at school. I don't remember the dance or the date but I do remember the house. It wasn't grand but nearly new and large enough to invite two students for a weekend.

One of the conditions of my scholarship was that I pass all subjects with at least a "c". General Physics was mostly common sense with some math thrown in. I found it almost easy. I could pass Spanish and Math, but it took time. I was never good at dates and names in history and my slow reading had always made it difficult, but now I had a history professor who lectured all of this material and he was interesting in addition. For me the major struggle was English composition. Dr. Ball's last gig on his final exam was to give a choice of three topics for a composition, two of which were "A Duck's Place in Society" and "How to Name a Tugboat".

Sophomore Summer

Soon, I was back on the farm and it was summer. This was another reality. I got the plowing done for corn and waited to hear from Mr. Kelly about the Federal Inspector job which could provide cash for room and board next year, and then there was the house. These first two were givens, essentials, the third was optional — at least to my father.

The house had been my priority since we had moved back from the modern house on the bigger farm.[26] I had gotten my father to agree in principle but not in timing. We had cut some pine logs on the mountain land we owned in Virginia and he had them sawed into two-by-fours. They were stacked to cure

---

[26] Glen always referred to this house as "Ridgeway." Berkeley County Historical Society says it was built in1842 and is known in some historical records as The James Nathaniel Burwell House. It was later painted yellow. It is said to have changed sides 12 times in the Civil War. As a child I played in the front hallway where a large plaster scar was said to have been the result of a Civil War cannonball. It is located on Route 11, five miles south of Inwood, near the Virginia and West Virginia state line. - Editor

Ridgeway as it appeared when the family first moved in. The kitchen he renovated is on the left. The house was later painted yellow.

behind the smokehouse.

The loft over the kitchen was not a full story high. The rafters had been made from long hand hewn pine poles but these had been tied together at their centers by the joists of the partial ceiling. Over the years the poles had warped and this had pushed the center of the west wall out at the top. The kitchen ceiling sagged at the center but had seemed stable. To correct this we would have to tear down and rebuild the west wall.

I had drawn out the plan. We would rebuild this part to two full stories. The large kitchen (24x26 feet) would be divided into a modern kitchen with built-in cabinets and sink, and a utility room for the washing machine. The old stairway would be moved over between the rooms. I had always wanted a house with a front and back stairs. The upstairs would be divided into a new master bedroom, bathroom and hallway. The hallway would connect the new second story to the old existing house, ending at the first landing on the house's main staircase.

My father objected to two features. Raising the roof meant joining into the old slate roof on the main "L" and extending the back hall to the main hall meant cutting a door through two brick walls of the old house. Also, since the floors were at different levels, the bit of floor that turned into the front hall would have to be suspended in a box in the ceiling of the dining room and boxed off through my bedroom. I was determined. We were at an impasse.

So, at least, to get started, I went to the loft over the kitchen and started prying up the floor boards in what was then an unused part of the house. As it turned out, this small and rather innocent start, set the timing and commitment sooner and more firmly than even I had hoped. With only a few floor boards removed, the ceiling began to crack and pieces of plaster began falling into the kitchen. It seemed the two center joists had been pulled out of their sockets in the tilted wall and were only being held up by the nails of the floor which I was removing. I soon saw I had already gone too far. The kitchen ceiling was falling in. I couldn't fix it.

I dreaded my father's reaction. Perhaps he was overwhelmed. He looked very upset, but he didn't say much. He helped me move the refrigerator, table and kitchen cabinet into the dining room. He had accepted the inevitable.

After that, I continued to demolish the kitchen and as I got to the roof, he joined in. We tore down the west wall brick by brick. We cleaned off the old soft mortar and stacked the bricks to face the new structure. The foundation of this wall was removed down to ground level and a little below. Here, there was still stone carefully fitted together, solidly held together by the earth itself. My father started constructing a wooden form to pour concrete for the new foundation. I objected. I wanted the wall to be stone like the other part of the foundation. He thought this was ridiculous and said he wouldn't pay stone masons.

In desperation, I started fitting stone together against the face of the form using the stones from the old foundation. It might work. My father watched. He said it would weaken the wall and he wouldn't have it. I finally convinced him he could pour the concrete behind the stones, that it would fill in all the spaces between the stones and be just as strong. He thought it was silly to do all of this. I continued fitting the stones. It was difficult. I wanted it to match the other foundation. The job went on and on into the late evening.

The next morning when we started pouring the concrete most of the stones were still in place but a few had to be lifted up and held in place as the concrete was poured in behind them. When the form was removed the next morning, there was a problem. The concrete had filled in but it had also formed splotches of concrete across the face of the stones. I got a chisel and a hammer and tried knocking those unsightly pieces off. The concrete was still green and it went better than I had expected. The spill-overs peeled off the stones and run-troughs were cut back to look like mortar. It was beautiful.

The bricklayers came. They chose to use hollow core cinderblocks faced off with the old brick. When they got up to the windowsill level, mother came out into the yard and watched as the bricks began to go up beside the kitchen window.

"I think there ought to be two windows there," she said.

"They've already laid the bricks," my father objected.

"But only on that side," I offered. "We could put another one over there."

The extra window was added using a window frame we had already purchased for an upstairs, and I went to town to get another window.

We were able to reset the joists for the upstairs floor in the new wall . We moved the old stairway and its tongue-and-groove wall over to form the utility room. The refrigerator would fit in a recess under the steps. We laid down boards as a temporary upstairs floor, put in the ceiling joists, rafters and then the roof sheeting. While we were putting up the interior walls, I stepped backwards on the loose boards and fell through the floor. I struck my side on the way down. It hurt. I went into shock, freezing cold and shaking. I was scared.

When we reached the doctor, I found out I had cracked my ribs. Once they were taped, the pain was manageable, but I was sore for a while.

We had planned to pour the floors in the kitchen and utility room as concrete slabs. This meant the wiring, pipes, and heat ducts had to be planned and laid out. I ran electrical cables, as well as hot and cold water pipes across the floor that would run up to the bathroom and the sewer through the outside wall. I roughed-in the electrical cables for the lights, switches, and receptacles.

A couple of years before, I had jacked up the furnace from the clay floor (which had probably once been brick) and poured a concrete floor under it and then a floor for the coal bin. I recovered the furnace and my father had tinsmiths make boxes for heat ducts into the dining room and the living room.

I had repaired the fireplace in my bedroom by replacing the bricks that had been removed in the earlier furnace installation. I had then taken a picture reading by the fire *(à la* Lincoln). I had repaired the hearth and mantel in the living room. The hearth had sunk, breaking the bricks, due to a leak of the powdered clay in the box supporting it. I replaced this then I went to work on the mantel. It was rather fancy. It had pieces that were loose and pieces missing. With the crude tools I had, I tried to duplicate these as best I could to restore it to its original design. We used that fireplace occasionally.

Now, I ran a heat duct into the floor of the kitchen, one up the wall to the bathroom and a return air duct back to the furnace. I joined the return ducts to a large tin box behind the furnace. In the box, I had mounted a truck fan driven by a belt from a motor on top. This would now be a forced air furnace.

We poured the floors in the kitchen and the utility room. Then we replaced the roof over the back porch. We had finished the outer shell of the house.

All in all, it was a rough summer. I had still worked my midnight to 8 a.m. shift as an inspector and was then off into the evening to work on the house.

We ordered the bathroom fixtures from Sears. They were shipped by train and we picked them up from the station at Inwood. Dad promised to get Uncle Tull to do the plumbing for the bathroom and Uncle John would bring out a crew and build the kitchen cabinets and do the finish work. He only promised to knock the holes through for the hallway if Uncle John thought it would work.

Glen kept his Hallicrafters radio at his bedside and it still worked when he passed away in 2016.

My brother had loaned me a little plastic radio that first year, with instructions where to hit it when it dropped out. I had found the shorted tube and replaced it, but I wanted my own, something more technically impressive. Hallicrafters, which had formerly only made communication equipment, was making a bid for the popular market, and had made a little S-38. It was just a six-tube ac/dc but it would tune three short wave bands and had a band spread dial. It was in a dark green metal box with lots of knobs and switches. It sold for $49. In the last few days of the summer I showed it to my father. He said, "Is that what you really want?" I said it was. He bought it for me.

It was fall and I had to go back to school.

Sophomore Year

For my Sophomore year I was assigned a room in the dorm. I was surprised and elated. By this time, I knew that the great shortage of housing for the men was compounded by the increase in enrollment at Westhampton (the women's college). The school thought the women had to be provided with housing on campus so one of the men's dormitories was given over to the women.

That summer the school had constructed temporary housing out of reconstructed army barracks— complete with double decker bunks. They were pretty awful. I was fortunate to get a room in Jeter Hall. I initially thought it was just my turn, but

Jeter Hall, University of Richmond

after I met my new roommate Sam, I heard him mutter to his friend, when they thought I was out of ear shot, "He don't look like a football player to me." I figured later he must have tried to get his friend as a roommate and was unsuccessful. It did occur to me that my campus job gave me friends in the administration office which may have helped me get a room in Jeter. I didn't know, and, of course, I didn't ask. Sam was a senior. He was alright but he was an economics major. We had nothing to talk about.

I must have been asked to help in the Deans office that year to help make up the class rosters at the beginning of the term. I wrote my mother that I worked until two o'clock, but it was OK because they were all so nice to me. This year the chapel slips had been changed and now it took only about half as long

207

to record the attendance. No one gave me anything else to do on a regular basis and I figured I deserved the time off as a reward for my good management.

In the 1940's the U.S. Post Office was considered a modern miracle. To people living in the country, it was a godsend. You could order from a catalog, from a faraway city, and have it back in a week. Rural Free Delivery, like the Rural Electrification Act, was a gift. And the Post Office — neat, clean, and efficient — represented the Federal Government to the people. The Postmaster was a desirable government job and highly respected. Even when the Post Office was only the corner of a little country store, it was a formal, orderly corner and you respected it.

I mention this because the Post Office was very friendly to college students. Not only were letters three cents and postcards one cent (and that was the card and the postage) but there were laundry mailers. It could be a cardboard box as long as you declared it as laundry with no personal correspondence inside, but Sears sold a laundry mailer. It was a simple fiberboard box, riveted at the corners, made in two halves and held together with a fiber strap with a slip buckle. Its most ingenious feature was a slide out address card which was just flipped over for the return trip. You paid by the pound but two weeks laundry was only a little over a dollar.

In the middle of the Sophomore year automatic washers were installed in the basement of Jeter Hall. For a dime you could do a whole load of wash. It was soap-suds-on-the-floor and cross-dyed-shorts to begin with, but we learned. Then I only sent my shirts home. I can't remember that there were dryers. I do remember socks hanging on a string in the room.

There was a student activities building behind Jeter Hall. It was one of the temporary buildings, made of wood, and in poor condition. It had two ping pong tables and an old piano. It was a place to hang out. I met kids from New York, some Jewish. It was interesting to talk and compare backgrounds and points of view. I made several friends, people I could talk to and go to for help with homework.

Lon Ussery was one of these friends. He was from Wilmington, North Carolina. He was friendly with my Spanish buddies, but I don't think he considered himself part of the band. In fact, he once kidded me for looking like "the great white father" in this group. I was a head taller and my hair was bleached out. It was close enough to be funny. Lon would invite me to study with him. He was an A+ student and these sessions were very one sided with him explaining the material to me. I told myself it was the interesting questions I would ask but it may have been charity or just pity.

That year I rigged telephones on a party line with Api, Bobby, and Peter Cam. Peter was Chinese from Hong Kong. He had a car. The phones were toys and took a bit of applied physics to make them work.

I had begged my mother in each card and letter to give me complete progress reports, step-by-step, on the house projects. Mother's reports were too vague for my detailed interest and I had no way to project when it would be finished. I had no way to help. I felt out of control and I was embarrassed not to have an indoor bathroom. I had already asked Api to come home for Christmas.

That second year some of us could buy beer legally, could fake it, or knew somebody who could fake it. Peter had a car and we'd pile in and go off to a tavern that was near the campus but too far to walk. We'd drink two or three beers and this was enough to put most of us in an almost falling down stupor.

Then there was the night when some of us went with Peter to Washington, DC. I'm not sure if I was one of them, but I remember a long, long ride into the dark, the white dome of the Capital Building, against the black sky, walking around the deserted parking lot on the east face and the long, long drive back to Richmond. As I said, I'm not sure I actually went, I may be remembering someone else's account of that night. I don't remember if Peter drank and I don't remember worrying about it.

When my usual birthday cake arrived, I invited several of the guys in to cut the cake. I don't remember the details, but there were some six packs of beer and a block of ice. Cake and beer are a terrible combination, but who can account for college kids? The block of ice was placed in a trash can and the beer packed around it. The whole thing was covered with newspaper pushed down around the ice. The cake was cut and passed around. We must have each had a couple of beers but this qualifies as a toot in a Baptist college. Maybe I had a third.

I woke up the next morning startled by a knock on the door followed by a key in the lock.   As I attempted to sit up, I was disappointed to realize I was late and had already missed breakfast. I never missed breakfast!

Mrs. Johnson, the boys' housemother, entered my room. I had never seen her in anyone's room before. In fact, I had hardly seen her at all. I don't know what I was wearing but I didn't attempt to get out of bed. The trashcan was still in the middle of the floor. The ice had melted and the soggy newspaper covered, what I assumed, was more beer.

She sat down and said, "Mr. Whitacre, are you alright?"

"I'm alright. I just woke up late."

The trashcan was setting there like a volcano protruding through the floor but she never looked directly at it. In fact, she looked past it as if it wasn't there. "Well, I just wanted to be sure you were alright."

She paused. It seemed like forever before she was finally got up and walked back to the door. "Now you are sure you're alright, Mr. Whitacre?"

"Yes, yes, I'm fine." She left.

I sat for moment on the side of the bed. She must have known. She must have known what was in the can. I lifted out the wet newspaper and was relieved there were no beer cans left. There were beer cans in the other trashcan. I went downstairs for a quick shower and went to my next class.

At the time it seemed Mrs. Johnson had done nothing at all. But I realize now, what she didn't do was the most effective of all. We never did that sort of thing again and in the years ahead we seemed to have grown out of the idea of drinking to get drunk.

By the middle of the second year I had collected a number of pictures of the campus. They were moody, taking advantage of the play of light on the buildings and the trees. It occurred to me to make up a catalog with order blanks, pass it around and see if I could get any orders.

I had found a closet in the basement of Jeter

Hall which was piled with junk. Mrs. Johnson gave me a key and permission to clean it out. I was taking Spectroscopy[27] that semester and could have used the physic lab's darkroom, but this closet was all mine and I could use it any time day or night.

I got orders. Boy, did I get orders! Not being a capitalist, I think I had based the prices on the cost of paper and developer. I had ignored labor, artistic ability, and the now familiar greed. It was a lot of work and I was sick of the whole thing by the time I had filled all of the orders.

Then, later in the second semester, I noticed a single room across the hall was vacant. I went directly to the administration office to enquire if I could switch rooms. I got permission and moved.

I soon understood why the room was vacant. It had no heat. The campus had a huge heating plant in a separate building off on one edge of the grounds and the heat was distributed by underground steam pipes. This room was a tiny piece of this mammoth system but no one could make it work.

I set out to make myself a heater. Using the metal shade from a desk lamp I found in the junk pile behind the student activities building and a heating

---

[27]Theory of spectrographic analysis and study of various types of spectrographs. A spectrograph is an instrument that separates light by its wavelengths and records this data. Lab work in qualitative analysis.

coil I bought from the dime store, I made a radiant heater. It was, of course, both a fire and an electrical hazard but if you placed it under the desk and wrapped your robe across the front of the desk, it was a cozy way to study.

I had invited Api home for Christmas, but now I became more and more worried. As nearly as I could tell, they had joined the roof into the old part of the house and cut through the walls to join the back hall to the front hall. This had worked out well and was completed but the bathroom still wasn't finished.

It was nearly Christmas break. I had to tell Api I would prefer that he come home on spring break. I didn't explain why. I realized this was being unkind to him but explaining why would have been more unkind to me.

Rafael "Api" and Glen

With the work I did over Christmas vacation, the bathroom was finished by spring break. Api came home with me on

214

the bus and my father picked us up in Winchester. Finally, after twenty years I had a home I could invite a friend to.

Now that this was accomplished, I realized I had not thought beyond this goal. With the commitment to the house, I had no social life for years. With Api there, something of that ilk seemed required. We went to the local rollerskating rink. I spent most of the evening just trying to remain vertical but Api met a girl. She had gone to my high school and was a couple of years younger. She was quite taken with Api and was interested in a date the next day. I had never had a little black book, but I was able to invite the girl's older sister and the four of us went to Virginia the next day to see the caves at Endless Caverns.

Mother fed and pampered both of us in every way she could. I think Api enjoyed himself but it was more stressful for me than I had expected.

When the time came to pay deposits on our rooms for the next year, I definitely did not want to keep the cold room. I knew Api's roommate was graduating but I assumed he would ask his brother, Orlando, who had been stuck in the temporary housing that year. Then one day Api asked me if I would like to sign up for his room. I said, "I thought you would ask Orlan."

"No, he doesn't have the priority."

"Oh, I didn't know. Well, sure, I'd love to."

"We can go over to the office and sign up then."

I wondered about the "priority" thing. After all, I had gotten in to Jeter Hall as a sophomore. I figured Api and his brother had their reasons and I wasn't going to fight it. I loved that room.

Api had bought a motor bike that year, or rather a motored bicycle is more accurate. It was a bicycle with a small motor. It had no gears and it needed direct powerful help from the peddles to start off. Api rode around the campus a few times. I rode it downtown once but stop lights, trucks and street cars were too much. I didn't try it again. I thought it was a bad choice but he hadn't ask me so I didn't comment. I volunteered to keep it for him over the summer. I thought it might be great on country roads.

Bringing Api's bike home gave me an excuse to have the car on campus for the last week of school. I began writing letters to my mother in a campaign to convince my father. Then I had to squeeze in a trip home during final exams to pick up the car. This led to some frantic, even registered, letters home.

Once I had the car on campus, it was so novel that I drove it downtown and, by force of habit, took the trolley back to the campus. An hour or so later, I remembered and had to take the trolley back to pick up the car.

It was a fun week. We drove out to the quarry and swam in the warm spring sun. Palling around in this mix of new freedom, and the pressure of final exams, absorbed a lot of adrenalin that week. It was great.

When the car was packed for home, I had not exaggerated the load. The back seat, trunk and half of the front seat were full.

As to the bike in open country, I rode it once to "my hill". The bike wasn't much fun, it was too slow.

Junior Summer

Summer brought the now usual routine of plowing and planting, working forty hours a week at the Inspector job, and later in the summer, hay making. Also, there were things to do around the house but now, for the first time I felt I could live in my house and not just build it. It was a vacation compared to the summer before.

I had bought a used record changer in the last few days at college. I modified the Hallicrafters radio by adding a phono plug. The changer was an old Webcor designed to play only 78's. I wanted to convert it to play the new LP's.

I worked out the mechanics. I calculated the size of the motor drive diameter to reduce the turntable speed to 33 1/3 rpm. The mechanics to shift the idler from one drive surface to the other was built and it worked. The more difficult task of making the smaller drive surface was tricky. I found a piece of brass tubing a little larger than needed and soldered it to the end of the motor shaft. This was done by guesswork and it would, of course, be somewhat off center. My first doubt was if the solder would hold to the steel shaft. It held.

I was committed now. I placed a file against the frame of the changer to get a perpendicular surface, and with the motor running very slowly, I eased the file against the brass tubing. When I was certain the file was making contact for the whole revolution, I put the turntable in place, placed an object on the surface and counted the number of revolutions in one minute. Success! It was a little greater than 33 1/3. Now I just needed to continue the filing to reach the right speed.

The pickup arm had been designed for about one ounce of needle pressure. An ounce is twenty-eight grams. The standard, then, for the LP was about ten grams. I rigged a coil spring in the arm pivot to reduce the pressure and bring it into range.

Then it was off to Winchester to buy an LP recording. Somewhat to my surprise, I selected Bizet's

Carmen with Rise Stevens and Raoul Jobin. Some years later, when one of my New York Sophisticates saw the cover, he said he thought it was a rather weak performance. Well, maybe, but I had made an LP player and that was the first thing I had heard it play.

The four-inch speaker in the little metal box of the Hallicrafters did not do justice to Bizet. I wanted a bigger speaker so I upgraded to a six-inch one. I then got some walnut boards, had them planed, and built a cabinet to accommodate the changer and the speaker. To top it off, literally, I rigged a mercury switch inside an electric clock as a radio wake up.

I think it was this summer that my brother added the second section onto his house, adding the cistern, basement, kitchen, bed room, bath and two porches. My father had given him the old storehouse on the land we owned back on the mountain. We tore that down and used that lumber for most of the addition.

There was one oak 2x4 in the south wall that no nail would penetrate. He had a student helping him that summer and we'd watch as he'd reach that stud with each piece of sheeting. There was a clear line of bent over nails all the way up the wall. I helped him as much as I could that year. It was my brother's newly acquired joiner that I used to build my speaker cabinet.

So, with three jobs and a hobby, the summer went by fast. I had accumulated $300 + for first semester's room and board from my Inspector's job, and with the my new record player, it was off to my Junior year.

Junior Year

Getting that walnut phonograph cabinet up to the fifth floor of Jeter Hall was not easy but everything about the tower room was great. It was actually inside the roof with two dormers looking out at right angles. The east side had four windows and the south, two.

Jeter Hall had been built in the 30's and initially the bathrooms and showers were all in the basement. The floors were concrete, cold and never seemed quite clean. Sometime later, possibly due to an increased interest in bathing, little baths had been added in odd little shapes and places. Since the plumbing had been added, you had to step up into these but the floor and walls were all white ceramic tile. They were small and functioned mostly as a one man operation. There was one of these baths on the fifth floor of the tower and since there were only two rooms at that level it was nearly a private bath. Also, the gravity heating system favored the upper floors, and this, being the most upper of floors, was always warm.

We had a housemother who had a room in the

dorm and would be available, I guess, if you had a problem or wanted to talk to her. There was also rudimentary maid service. They emptied the trash cans, swept the floor and made the beds each day. They would also dust the tops of things if they were not too cluttered. Sheets, pillow cases and blankets were your own responsibility. After the automatic washers were installed this was much easier.

By the end of my Sophomore year, my faculty advisor was from the physics department. He had seen me work in the physics lab and in one session he asked me if I would like to work in the Physics Department for my scholarship. The answer was a resounding, "Yes, please!" The job there was to draw the equipment and set up the lab experiments each week. I had to track the schedule for each class and have the equipment ready for each session. It was great. I had access to the big patch board in the power room and could plug any voltage into any plug in the building. But better, I had keys to the building. I could come and go at will, even on Sunday afternoons when I could be all alone (in the physics labs).

The freedom did trip me up once. On the spur of the moment, I went home one week end and got back late Sunday night. My second period on Monday was in the Physics building. I was met in the hall by my professor.

He looked disturbed, "What happened?"

I had forgotten. I cut the next two periods to get caught up.

Api brought back a message from his parents to thank me for taking care of his things over the summer and he asked me to come to visit at Christmas. I had never thought of being away from home at Christmas before. I did want to go but I could not imagine asking my father for the airfare. I thanked Api but said I couldn't come. This was a decision I have regretted the rest of my life. I had not fought for it. I did not even try.

That year, the tower room was the crossroads and hangout for all of the foreign students. Now, there were five Chinese students. Two were from the interior of China. They roomed together but didn't speak Chinese to each other; they spoke different dialects. They had both studied Mandarin but that, too, was a foreign language, so they spoke English to each other. This was the era of Chiang Kai-shek and they were concerned about the safety of their families. Often they had to delay paying their school fees because of the difficulty of getting gold out of the country. To me it seemed strange to think of the family's wealth as pieces of gold.

Two were from Hong Kong. Peter was one of the gang, spoke English well and had a great sense of humor. The other, I thought, was a jerk. I didn't like his ideas or his attitude toward people. One day, when he opened the drawer of his desk, I noticed there were several packages of nylons in the back. I wondered if he thought these would be legal tender for girls in America. I didn't say anything.

He had a very expensive camera. It had a metal focal plane shutter which he had managed to damage. He wanted me to fix it. I didn't attempt that but I did agree to take it to a camera shop to get an estimate. When they told me it would be $60, up front, just for the estimate, I brought it back. I don't know what happened to that camera, or that guy.

There were also five Spanish students, Api, Orlan, George, Carlos and Paco. Paco was a graduate student, two or three years older, more reserved and stable than the other guys. He had hopes of being a radio announcer in New York and when he put on his radio voice his diction was so clear and precise, even I could understand his Spanish. His English had less accent than the other guys, but it was still clearly there. Paco was a great guy.

The only meeting with a Spaniard whose accent nearly fooled me had occurred the year before when, very early one Sunday morning, there was a knock at my door. When I got the door open there was a rather disheveled young man in a suit. He said he was

Glen (on right) with college buddies

stranded from the night before and wanted a nickel to make a phone call. It struck me that he wanted a nickel — he didn't ask to borrow or for change. But it was only a nickel so I gave him one. He thanked me and disappeared. As I thought about it, I thought there was an accent, just a tiny bit. I told the guys about this and they said that it must be Chico. He was a doctor, an intern, at the medical college downtown. They knew him and said he didn't have an accent. How he got stranded near the girls dorm (the one taken over from the boys) on a Sunday morning with no money, we could only imagine. They were not surprised.

The comings and goings in the tower room were often noisy and confusing but interesting and very satisfying to me. We went shopping for records and in those days you selected a record from a counter and then listened to it in a booth. They made some interesting selections. I couldn't afford many records so we pooled our purchases. I had the record player. Conversations between the Spaniards were still in Spanish but they spoke English to the Chinese and to me. I could use Spanish phrases but I was never able to master a conversation.

I had signed up for Conversational Spanish the second year but when I reported for class, there was only me and the professor. After a while, he looked up and grinned and said, "Well, I guess we will have to call this off."

I told myself it was for economic reasons, that a professor couldn't teach one student, but then he had been my Spanish teacher the year before. Perhaps, it was just his realistic evaluation of the situation.

At one of our many bull sessions, I was told I should have the nickname, "Gallego". Then they explained that a *gallego* was a fellow from Galicia, the province on the north coast of Spain. It seemed that, through the ages, Norsemen had left large deposits of blonde hair and blue eyes there. In the south, where the Greeks, Romans, Gauls, and Moors had come and gone these had become what we now call Latin. To the Latin, a *gallego* was very "square" and had no sense of rhythm. I was pleased, even flattered at their accurate observation. I said they were exactly right.

We all laughed and the name didn't stick.

Although the crowd was dominantly "foreign", there were other mutual friends, too. One day as a confab was breaking up, one of Api's friends stayed behind and when Api went out of the room he said, "Our fraternity would like to invite you to become a member."

I had never really considered a fraternity and my surprised response was, "Oh!"

He went on, "I waited until Api left because our fraternity doesn't accept foreign students."

My response was knee jerk and unthinking, "Then you don't want me."

He was shocked and then looked angry. He left.

The room always cleared out in the evening and Api and I would study at our desks at opposite extremes of the room. I had to study late a lot and I had moved my desk out into the small dormer. I usually had 8:30 classes and I always went to breakfast. My loss of sleep would seem to accumulate over the week and sometimes after my 8:30 class on Saturday, I'd go back to bed and sleep until the late afternoon. I'd find myself alone and hungry. I'd dress as warmly as I could and strike off the mile and a half to the village to get fruit and crackers. I'd make it back for supper at school and keep most of what I bought for snacks during the week.

I understood, but never forgave, the attitude of Api and the others had toward fruit. Api would gulp down a tangerine and then another. I knew they were just something that grew in their backyard at home, but to me they were something special, something to be savored slowly.

I rigged a way to heat soup with an old hot plate I had repaired and a one half gallon coffee can. We would sometimes have soup late at night. I later got a popcorn popper.

As time went on and we knew we could trust each other, we could talk about things on a somewhat deeper level. He told me that his hometown, Manati, was very small and that the people around the town were mostly poor. He said his father was likely to be paid for his medical services with a live chicken.

We still differed on the "good girl/bad girl" point of view but I had begun to understand how this was tied to his religion and I didn't think I should criticize his religion. I expected the same courtesy. Api said that there was no color discrimination in Puerto Rico. He admitted there was a strong class system based on family and wealth. As a group we usually sat in the back of the trolleys, among the blacks or behind the blacks. We meant this as a sign of equality and the conductors never objected. I've since wondered how the blacks saw this at the time. Did they understand?

Or was there something else we didn't understand?

He would never let me use the second person, the familiar voice, in Spanish. He said that was for family and for servants. He didn't explain it beyond that. When I came back one fall I greeted him with, "Compadre!"

He said, "No, no, don't say that. That's the way the uneducated, the country people talk."

He did, finally, compliment me on my accent. He said I was different from the other Americans. Then he proceeded to mimic the bad pronunciation of several words.

During that winter, Orlan, Api's brother, got a bad case of the flu. It was serious enough for the campus doctor to put him in the infirmary. The doctor's office was in the gymnasium but the infirmary was a room on the lower level of Jeter Hall. The doctor would visit once a day but there were no nurses. Care, I guess, was the responsibility of the housemother but we thought it was first our responsibility. We brought him his meals and books and stopped by just to be there.

Orlan had a problem with his eyes. Api had explained to me thst it was a defect inherited from his father. The eyelids do not develop completely and don't cover the eye. This causes part of the surface of the eye to dry out. The eyes are constantly irritated and badly blood shot. Orlan was very self conscious of this and wore aviation-style, dark glasses all the time, except, of course, when he slept. When I would come into the room I would pick up his glasses and hand them to him without looking directly at him. I meant this as an act of kindness to avoid his embarrassment. Later, I thought it was like saying, "I don't like to look at your ugly eyes." I have always wished I had talked this out and come to an understanding.

This was the 40's and everybody smoked, especially college boys and especially in the south. It was in the air. I, too, joined in. I had never smoked at home. My brother didn't smoke and my father only smoked a cigar occasionally. Cigarettes were only 16 cents a pack and at first I could stretch a pack for a week. It made you one of the guys and gave you something to do with your hands during social encounters. Unfortunately it was habit forming and I continued on for seven or eight years until my son was crawling. I finally made myself stop.

Once I had gotten English, History and most of my language requirements behind me, I took a philosophy course and a psychology course. It seems I did not treat the question, "Do we really exist?" with the proper gravity and got a poor grade on my term paper. Initially, I was fascinated by treating human behavior in a scientific manner but bogged down near the end of the course. This left Chemistry, Math and Physics. I did alright in Chemistry but I didn't like the lab because they didn't provide stools to sit on like the physics labs. I had had to take a high school algebra course and this had put me a year behind in math for my physics courses. Consequently, I did not do as well as I had hoped in electronics and thermodynamics. I never did understand complex numbers. I liked electronics lab. From scratch, I built a read/write head for recording on magnetic tape and an oscillator and amplifier to drive it. It worked.

I had volunteered, somewhere along the way, to ride herd on the PA system in the chapel on those days that I had to attend. I could enter the side door past the glass cabinet containing the over-arm record cutting lathe. I never knew who it belonged to or if it was ever used, but the idea of seeing it used or using it myself fascinated me. The job was kind of fun, I felt part of the production. I sat in the choir loft, behind the rail, and peeked over to keep up with the program. Just check the mic, turn on the power, ride the volume and turn it off when you leave. One day there was a problem — the sound of the person speaking began to drop out. I fiddled around with the cables to the amplifier hoping to find a loose connection. I accidentally touched the grid cap of the first stage. My buddies in the audience swore fire came out of the speakers. After the program, my faculty advisor came up and helped me remove the amplifier. Then carrying the amplifier with its wires dangling, I went to the speaker and apologized (that is to the man — not the mechanism).

In February, I got a letter from my sister-in-law Virginia. It said my father was ill. She said it was serious and that he was being taken to Baltimore for treatments. Mother hadn't told me anything about this. Apparently, it had been developing for some time but mother hadn't told me. I wrote mother frantically, asking for an explanation. I don't remember how I was told, or how long it took to find out that my father was being taken to Baltimore for radium treatments. Yes, it was cancer, cancer of the lymph nodes. The treatment would slow down the progress but we were given no real hope for a cure. The treatments made him sick but he was able to continue his school bus job and some work on the farm.

I think my reaction was just to be numb. I guess it was too big to face. I just pushed it back and left it to think about it later. There was, too, the very selfish reaction I had to live my own life.

The month before I had asked my father to put another $50 in the bank to make up the $240 I needed to pay my room and board for the last semester. I had bought my tuxedo for the Junior Prom with money I'd put aside for that purpose and was waiting for my income tax rebate. My letters did tell my father to take it easy, but that was about it.

Somewhere, along here, my memory lost its sense of time. The next two years consist of individual events. It takes some considerable effort to form these into anything as formal, or as linear, as time. Surely, spring followed winter and fall followed summer, but just how, why and when remains a jumble.

Then there was a girl. A girl named Ethel. A girl I met at a dance. She liked me. I had girl friends before, that is friends that were girls, but they were always committed to someone else. For the few times I had picked a girl and advanced the situation, I had been rebuffed, early and soundly. But she liked me. She was a nurse, a professional person, a serious person. But she liked me. I was busy, I already had too many complications. I didn't need any more commitments. But she liked me. She was pretty. I liked to touch her. I liked to show her off to my friends. I was failing differential equations. But she liked me. And when I didn't call her for a long time, she was still there. She liked me.

We went to movies and walked in the parks and ate at White Tower. Neither of us had any money. I didn't go to her graduation and I regret that. I had a thermodynamics exam. It was a take home, open book exam typed on a half page. I looked at it and assumed I could take it in one day. It took a week, and I barely passed it. But I should have gone to her graduation. I've always regretted that.

Glen and Florence Ethel McNeal

Sometime that semester, I was informed by my faculty advisor that I was a candidate for the Honors Physics Society. You had to have maintained a "B" or better average in Physics. I was flattered and did join, although that was another $15 for initiation fee and key. Then they elected me Secretary. I can't remember doing very much as secretary and I didn't get the word and missed both group pictures for the yearbooks.

I wrote to my mother sometime during the winter that Api and Paco wanted to come home to the Apple Blossom Festival. I had told them about the two days of celebration and described it as a protestant Mardi Gras. I can't remember that they came, the dates probably didn't work out. I do have a picture of Paco with the old Reo truck on top of the mountain going to Glengary. I don't know why we would have been there unless we were getting a Christmas tree. Maybe he came home for Christmas.

My pictures were noticed and someone from the year book asked me if they could use some of them in the '49 issue. I was flattered and said sure. They wanted to know how much I wanted to use the pictures. (Well, again, just call me stupid.) I said, "No, no, just give me a byline. I'll loan you the negatives, you make the copies you want, then give the negatives back to me."

They made their copies and I got the negatives back. When the books were distributed, they were the feature pictures, four full pages right up front. They were beautiful. Then I looked for the subtle way they had given me my byline. It was indeed subtle, it wasn't there. And worse, the commercial photographer, possibly smarting by comparison, had taken a full page at the front of the ads section that announced, "Web Photographs by FOSTER STUDIOS." I had been robbed.

Api sold his motor bike sometime during that year. So when spring came and the end of second semester, I didn't have the same excuse to bring the family car down. But with the record player and all the extra stuff I'd collected over the year I came up with a strong argument for doing so.

The pressure of exams, the release of exams, the warm spring sun at the quarry — it was great. It was on one of these jaunts that some of us were sitting in the car waiting for the stragglers to show up and Julio said something to Api in English. He caught himself. Everyone stopped, then he said, in English, "I spoke to you in English." We all looked at each other, a little pensive and grinned.

There were several trips to the quarry and at least one of these sessions lasted long into the evening. When I came back to the car, the little green ammunition box that I had left on the floor in the back was missing. This box contained my camera and light meter. This camera had been purchased form Sears for $9.95, but this was not its value.

It had been my only camera through high school and college. At thirteen, I had made myself a tripod out of wood. It had a swivel head. I had bought a real electronic light meter, I had taken pictures of lightning that had gotten an honorable mention and a $5

Glen always had a camera

235

check in a national contest. I had taken the pictures of the campus that had sold. These pictures were to be featured in the '49 yearbook. I had a negative file of 106 rolls of film taken with this camera. It was gone.

Even worse, Paco's 35mm camera was in that box. I had borrowed it to take color slides. I felt responsible for losing his camera too. I talked to Paco and proposed that next year we buy a camera together and it would be his at the end of the year. He agreed.

Then as things were breaking up and goodbyes were being said a crew moved in to paint the dorm. They were looking for help. I could use the money. I volunteered. I was told the paperwork would take a while and it would have to be mailed to me. I took the job for a week. Commercial painting was not fun. Ignore small damage, paint over dirt, get it done. I did wrangle permission to paint the tower room and I did the best I could.

Senior Summer

That summer, I don't remember well. I know I plowed for corn and rigged a light on the Fordson tractor from the magneto so I could disk long into the night. My father still worked but we were cutting back. He knew how ill he was. We didn't talk about it.

I returned to my government job, but this time, when Mr. Kelly appeared, he had a new proposal. I was to be the supervisor over two inspection stations, the one at Harrisburg and the one at Culpepper. I would pick up a government truck each day from a garage in Winchester. The supervisor had to visit all three shifts in a pseudo random fashion and thus would have to work what amounted to the swing shift.

There was more paperwork and with the work on the farm, I could never get enough sleep. This is the only time I ever went to sleep while driving. I would be driving on the late night shift and suddenly realize I'd been asleep. Luckily, I didn't wreck the truck or hit anyone. The mountain roads were crooked but mostly deserted late at night. With the new job I was making $1.33 an hour and I kept it all for going back to school.

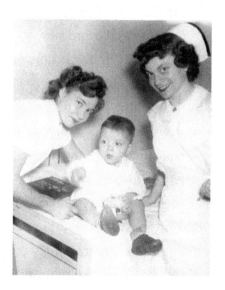

Ethel McNeal (right) at one of her early nursing jobs.

Ethel had taken a job in a hospital at The Medical College of Virginia, from which she had graduated. She and her classmate, Mary, had taken an apartment in a private home in the western part of Richmond. I visited a few times that summer, but it was a long way to drive. The landlady had arranged a room for me to stay over.

Senior Year

Moving back into the newly painted tower room for the Senior year, was pretty much the same deal. I brought the record player. It was the hangout for the guys and there was noise and confusion and laughter and Spanish.

Now I was down to my final two semesters and it was all math and physics. I had been working toward that end but little did I know that each physics course also had a two hour lab. There was lecture, experiments, and then lab reports to be computed and written up. The workload was unrelenting. It was the only time I ever, truly, worked all through the night. I finished just in time to turn the reports in at the 8:20 a.m. deadline.

Ethel continued working at the hospital and

living with Mary in the apartment in west Richmond. Mary had a steady beau and we double dated sometimes. We also had dinner at the apartment every now and then. The girls learned to cook excellent Spanish rice. Ethel came home with me at Christmas. Dad liked her Spanish rice too. She got along well with my mother

Glen, 1950

and my niece. I knew where this was going but I still avoided commitment until I had a job and could see a little distance ahead.

Sometime, during that year, a member of the marching band said the director wanted me to help make a recording. He took me to the gym where the band was assembling. It seemed an alumnus (from Greece, I think) had written a march and the band wanted to make a recording to be presented at some kind of ceremony.

I was shown the band's latest acquisition. It was an honest-to-God Brush tape recorder. This was all very new. I had never seen one. It was a reel-to-reel, one track, mono recorder using paper tape and had a "magic eye", from the old radio tuning days, as an indicator for recording level. It had one mechanical control, a multi function shifter lever, borrowed, I think, from a VW microbus. I helped set up the mic and adjusted the volume during the recording.

I learned fast. I loved this machine. Later I was asked to record a band concert in the Greek Theater. Then, I was asked to travel with the band and record a concert in an auditorium at another school.

After the concert there was a social given by the little old ladies. Going through a kind of receiving line, I was asked, "And what instrument do you play, son?"

I was taken by surprise and was embarrassed. The guy ahead of me piped up, "He plays the recorder."

She smiled and said, "I understand that is a very difficult instrument to play."

I nearly choked but just nodded and moved on. You see, I didn't know there really is an instrument called a recorder, an ancient form of the flute.

Then, someone from the student government came to me and said they wanted me to pick a public address system for the dining halls. I ordered a system: amplifier, mic and speakers, from Allied Radio. I also ordered a three speed record changer. I drew up plans for a cabinet and had it built in the wood shop. I also ran the wires under the floors of the dining halls and hung two speakers in each room.

As the spring vacation of our Senior year approached, Peter made a fascinating proposal. He suggested we drive up to New York for the week. So, Peter, Api, Orlan, Delio (a freshman) and I set off for New York. Peter had made arrangements to stay in a foreign student house in upper Manhattan near the George Washington Bridge. Grant's Tomb is there, too. I didn't know it was in New York, or that it was a real thing. It had always been the subject of Groucho's jokes.

We went to the top of the Empire State Building, saw Broadway, Times Square, Grand Central Station and rode the subway and the Staten Island Ferry. We climbed to the top of the Statue of Liberty including the arm and the torch. We were taken by a goodly number of tourist traps for the naive. These included having your picture taken at your table at a restaurant and being told you had to pay for copies before you could leave.

Peter took us all to dinner at a Chinese restaurant one night. Except for the large fish that watched me from the central platter all evening, it was very good and must have been very expensive for Peter.

One morning Peter and I found ourselves alone

at the hotel. When the others came back they said they had gone to Brooklyn. There was lots of locker room innuendo but they never, really, told us what they did or what happened.

So all went reasonably well until we were heading south on the Pulaski Highway just outside of New York in New Jersey. We stopped at a light and were hit in the rear by another car. We were hit hard enough to knock us into the car ahead of us. As a result, the grill was smashed in, the trunk lid was smashed, and the frame bent, buckling the body over the rear wheels. The rear bumper was knocked loose and was dragging.

No one was hurt, although Peter did have trouble with his neck later. Peter had the car towed, they exchanged insurance information and we were stranded.

With a very poor grasp of the geography, I proposed we take a bus to my home and have my brother take us back to Richmond. It was agreed and we scrounged up enough money for the bus fares. The thing I didn't realize was that the diversion west from Baltimore to Martinsburg and Ridgeway was almost as far out of the way as going directly to Richmond would have been.

I don't remember if this took overnight but we arrived at the end of my lane in Ridgeway in mid afternoon carrying suit cases, some broken, and walked the half mile down the lane to my house. We met my father shoveling manure out of the barn on the way. Mother fed us all and I went to talk to my brother.

He was not exactly pleased with the idea of driving to Richmond and back late into the night. His mood didn't improve as the night wore on and most of the conversation was in Spanish. We made it back in time for classes.

Then, very late in the year the band members came back and asked me to cut records from the tapes we had recorded as mementos for the band. I envisioned learning to use the overarm cutting lathe in the chapel. Instead I was told I would have to use an amateur swing arm cutter owned by the father of one of the band members.

I had to learn about acetate discs, cutting needles and editing tape. The ten inch discs would only hold about five minutes of recording time, so I had to rearrange the selections to fit on the discs. This meant cutting up the original master copy into little hunks, scattered over my room and then patching them back together with scotch tape. I got through all of this but then made one major misjudgment. I theorized that the frequency response of the recording would be improved if a shallower cut was made. To accomplish this I reduced the pressure on the cutting arm. I tried this and it worked well on my homemade record player. I then cut all of the discs. This was a major and time consuming job. When the records were passed out some came back and said the records wouldn't track on their players. It was then too late to correct the problem.

Then, very late in the year, Peter and I were sitting on the steps of the Physics Building. He said, "You have an uncle that can fix cars."

I didn't know what he meant. I may have told him I had an uncle that was an inventor who built things. "Well, he could fix cars, I guess. What do you mean?"

Peter said, "Glen, I am going to give you my car and your uncle can fix it."

I was startled. I knew I wouldn't ask my uncle to fix it. "You want to give me your car?"

"Yes, I give you my car."

It was a fascinating idea. "Well, how much will you take for it?"

"No, I give it to you."

It was a '42 Pontiac, eight years old, and it was badly wrecked. "No, you can't do that."

"Yes, I give it to you. I give you the papers and you go to New Jersey and get it."

He was grinning in his gleeful way. It actually seemed possible. I knew he had gotten a settlement from the insurance, they had paid me $16 for my suit case. "It's still in the garage in New Jersey?"

"Yes, I give you the address and the papers."

"OK, I should pay you something."

"No, I want you to have my car."

When it was time for the graduation, my mother and father came down. The service was held outdoors in the Greek Theater. The weather was beautiful. The day was beautiful. Familiar faces looked strange enrobed in long black gowns and silly mortar board hats with tassels. Then the music started and the parade of the faculty with their academic colors established the gravity of the occasion. The mechanics of marching down, line by line, shaking hands and being handed a certificate from the stack on the table seemed anticlimactic. We had been told not to worry if the certificate wasn't yours, we'll straighten that out later. Graduation was over. The feeling that it was real, that it was finished, and that it was sad began to register. The short congratulations seemed too short and superficial.

After the crowd had thinned out, and only little clumps of people were standing around talking, my father came up to me, when I was standing apart, and said, "Well, we made it." There were tears in his eyes.

I did not say it but my immediate internal response was, "We made it? I made it! With all the hard work, long hours in the summer, saving all of my money and the struggle to pass all of my subjects, it was, "I made it!" I still didn't say it and I hoped what I was thinking didn't show on my face. I think I said, "Yes, we made it."

I should, of course, have said much more. I should have said how thankful I was that he had given half of his cash income each year for my room and board. I should have said how sorry I was for relentlessly pushing and pushing to get the house rebuilt. I should have been more concerned with how he was managing to pay for the renovations and now his medical bills. I wish I had understood how sick he was and how he wondered if he could hang on until I graduated. I should have hugged him and cried too. I didn't. I regret this.

In thinking about this later, I remembered I had only seen my father cry at something unexpected (that is not a funeral, or something) one other time. When I was in high school there was a certain style of wrist watch that I wanted. It was the narrow, curved kind, only as wide as the band. I got one for my birthday, it was exactly what I wanted. They had given it to me at a meal in the kitchen with a birthday cake my mother had made.

I said I loved it and then went upstairs, got my old wristwatch and gave it to my dad. He had always carried a large and rather heavy pocket watch. He put it on and then he had tears in his eyes and kept turning away. Then, I didn't know if he was touched by my sudden gesture to give him my watch or if he was hurt by getting second best. Of course, I didn't ask him.

Then back at Jeter Hall, we packed the car with all of my stuff except one suitcase containing what I would need for my trip to New Jersey to get Peter's car. We said our goodbyes and they were off for home.

Api's brother had gone to Philadelphia a few days before to get the plastic surgery he needed to fix his eyelids. Api had stayed behind for graduation. The next day we took the train to Philadelphia and went to see Orlan.

He had both eyes done at the same time and was bandaged so that he was completely blind. He was in very good spirits. We helped him eat lunch and kidded around. I then said goodbye to both and headed off to New Jersey to pick up my car.

I found the garage. The car was in the junkyard. I showed the signed over title and said I'd come to pick up the car. After some fumbling they wrote me out a bill. It was for storage, $35. Peter, or the insurance, had paid the towing bill.

I counted my money, I had about $20. I said, "Well, I'll write you a check."

"We don't take checks."

"Well, I'll give you the cash I have and write a check for the rest."

"No, we don't take checks."

"Well, where is a bank I can get to?"

They told me how to get to a bank but the bank would not cash my personal check. I went to another bank. They wouldn't cash my check and explained that no bank in New Jersey would cash a personal check unless the person had an account with that bank and they verified that the account would cover the check. So, I begged them to call my bank, I would pay for it. They thought that was funny. I left the bank murmuring, as a kind of mantra, "Damn Yankees", over and over.

It was now late and my only choice was to go back to Philadelphia and get the money from Api. By the time I got bus connections and got there it was about ten o'clock at night. I knew Api was staying at the YMCA. I found it and asked for a room. I was told they were filled up. I then asked for the room number of Rafael Munoz-Noya. They couldn't give out that information.

I wandered off and sat down in the lobby completely baffled, still murmuring "Damn Yankees". After a while, I went to a pay phone and called the desk. The operator gave me Api's number. I went to his room and knocked. It took a while, he was asleep.

He came to the door, he invited me inside and I started to tell him what had happened. There was a knock at the door and a key turning in the lock. The guy from the front desk said I would have to leave. It was after curfew and guests were not permitted visitors after curfew. Api said he'd meet me in the lobby and I followed the guy back to the desk.

Api came down and I explained what had happened. He couldn't help me. He had gotten the tickets to go home that day and had paid his brother's hospital bill. His father had figured it very close and he only had a few dollars for food.

I was out on the street at eleven o'clock in a strange city with a suitcase and no idea where to go. I found a hotel in a couple of blocks and for $5, checked in. It was a long night. I couldn't call home because my family didn't have a phone. I had heard of wiring money but I didn't know how it was done.

The next morning I set out looking for a telegraph office. When I found one I asked if they could send money. They said, "Sure, how much do you want to send?" When I told them I wanted to receive money from my bank they were doubtful.

"I'll send them a telegram, then they can wire me money back."

"Yes, if they'll do it. I wouldn't."

"This is a small southern bank, I have an

account and my father has had an account forever."

"Well, it's your money."

"OK." I wrote out a message as short and concise as I could manage. He counted the words, I paid, and it was off.

Then I waited and waited and waited. I had sounded much more confident than I really was. Then, when it was almost four o'clock, and I was sure the bank had closed, the clerk called out my name. The money had come.

I made it back to the garage before it closed. I paid the money and got the keys. Now I could inspect the car to see if it would start and if I could drive it. It started, but one end of the back bumper was dragging on the ground. I surveyed the damage and looked for a temporary fix. By this time I was mad enough to go into the shop take tools from the bench and go out and bolt it together. No one stopped me. Then, it was getting dark. I tried the headlights — they worked, I pulled into the traffic on the Pulaski Highway heading south, still muttering "Damn Yankees".

I had no assurance, beyond my own determination, that I could make it home. There were no beltways in those days, I worked my way through Philadelphia and on into Baltimore. Somewhere on the west end of North Avenue I missed a turn and found myself at a dead-end in a park. I tried to shift into reverse. It wouldn't shift into reverse. It took some planning and a little pushing to get turned around. Finally, I was on US 40 west and heading for home. I got in just before it began to get daylight.

During the summer I found fenders, a trunk lid and a grill in junkyards. I had a garage straighten the frame and paint the damaged parts. I later rebuilt the motor and drove it for more than four years including the trip to Kitty Hawk, Naples, and Key West on our honeymoon.

Glen with his Pontiac

Epilogue

When I visited the campus a couple of years later, by chance, I met my faculty advisor walking across the campus. I was taken by surprise, and said the first thing that came to mind. I complained that I had sent a new pickup cartridge for the dining hall's record player to a current student named Chuck and he hadn't installed it. He said Chuck was like that. He then asked me what I was doing now. I told him I had a technical job working for the Army. I expected some positive feedback.

He said, "That's too bad, I thought you could do better than that."

Of course, you could say I missed the whole point of college. I know the conventional "wisdom" is that college is where you make the contacts, the "friends" that you exploit in your career. So, I missed the point. I never learned to associate with people I didn't like.

As to the value of college, I used the physics and mathematics. I did, still, have to learn to write, but now with the help of secretaries and editors, I made do. Most of the applied technical stuff I had to learn on the job or invent on my own. Now, I had ac-cumulated a solid base to build on.

I ended up spending my entire career working as a systems analyst for the Federal Government. I'd like to think I made a significant contribution to the technical field, and kept it grounded in some reality. But in the end, I had to learn that any individual's at-tempt to change the will of the Military Industrial

Complex would fail.

The history, the literature, the art were aspects well worth the time and effort, even if they were not of particular interest then or now or ever. You've been there, you've seen it, you know where it comes from. You won't be intimidated by it.

As to my personal quest for enlightenment, perhaps I didn't do any better here. I never understood my fascination with Spanish culture. I certainly did not approve of the macho stance of the Spanish male and his obsession with testing fate in "sports" that artificially push the individual to the edge of death. So structured, so wrapped up by the church, a church that I saw as ignoring man's God-given nature, and from this, creating many evil things. But I was, somehow at home, happy, submerged in this thick Spanish soup.

After some years of more mature cogitation on the Catholic Church I think I have come to understand the teachings that leads to these consequences, and maybe even to see why, for its time. At about the same point, I came to understand how the customs of any culture are a system of checks and balances. Changes imposed from without, even with the best of intentions, without the native wisdom and time for its counterpoint to develop, may well lead to chaos. There is a lot of that going around.

Tenant Run Orchards in Northern Virginia in the 30's and 40's
by Glen Whitacre

Glen's parents Holmes and Lottie Whitacre are on the right.

It takes many years to develop a productive fruit orchard, so I don't know who it was that planted and nourished the apple orchards in Northern Virginia before they were bought up by investors after the crash of '29. I don't know why the original owners were forced to give them up; perhaps it was the Hoover economy or the bank's foreclosure schemes. In the 16 years that my father worked as a tenant orchardist, the investors were a lawyer, a coal company, an insurance agent and the owner of a men's clothing store. None had any background in running an orchard and so relied on a tenant to be both the daily laborer and the manager for all of the details of day-to-day work.

Knowledge of an opening for a tenant orchardist for the coming year must have been spread by word of mouth. I don't think there was any formal register or advertising in the newspaper as the majority of prospective tenants would not have received or read a newspaper. So by some means, a tenant would meet with an investor and with a verbal agreement, and perhaps a handshake, he would agree to serve for a year starting the next first of March. This date was common to all locations and was chosen as a nominal beginning of the orchard season. This date was judged to be late enough to avoid the bad snows of winter since the tenant would be moving his family and all of his possessions to the specified "tenant house" on that day (come hell, snow, or high water).

In bargaining for the position, the salary to be paid was, of course, a factor. There was some leeway, with the rates running from perhaps $24 to $30 a month. This was a fairly stable rate recommended by the Byrd family, the largest orchard holders. The Byrds were an esteemed political family of Virginia who boasted a governor and an admiral famous for his North Pole expedition. The reigning "Poppa Byrd" is supposed to have said, "A dollar a day is enough for any man." (Though my friend and local historian

James V. Hutton insists this is a Herbert Hoover quote.)

Jim Hutton worked at one of Byrd's orchards and claims that Byrd paid 5 cents to pick a bushel of apples from a 20-foot ladder while some others paid only 3 cents. Some suspected the Byrd family of opposing the building of the first free high school in the area because they wanted to maintain uneducated, cheap labor. Whether this was true, Jim's personal knowledge working on Byrd's orchards and attending Byrd's worker picnics is credible.

In response to the obvious question, "How can a family live on $30 a month," this was possible because of the nature and abilities of the tenant candidates. As the English, Scots and Irish had pushed across the rich and pre-owned lands of Virginia, the Dutch and Germans had come down and settled in the Shenandoah Valley from Pennsylvania. Many had been forced onto the cheaper land that was the foothills of the Appalachian mountain range. This was shale land, not fertile or rich. It was hilly and covered with trees. For those individuals who were able to obtain and clear enough land for a hardscrabble farm there, it was necessary for that family to be almost totally self sufficient. Shelter, furniture, food and clothing were all produced at home. This included making the thread to weave the cloth and making the lye that was used for soap.

Typically, these were large families of ten or twelve children. As the boys grew up, married and had their own families, they needed to move away and find employment. From their background, any promise of money for their labor was enticing since payment for labor within a hardscrabble family was unknown. By the 30's, these individuals were second or third generation survivors, trained by necessity, in this self-sufficient style of life. It was the self-sufficiency of the tenant's family that was offered in his deal with the investor. This self-sufficiency would permit the family to exist under the conditions being offered by the investor.

The tenant's wife was the cornerstone of self sufficiency for the family. Her commitment, as well as the children's, was being purchased by that same $30 a month. Typically, the bargaining was done without the knowledge of the wife. So, on a cold day in March, she was to arrive with the truckload of their possessions, to a strange and usually unclean house, to make do as best she could while her husband rigged up a stove to get a fire started.

It was essential that the elements the tenant's family would need to support themselves be present in this new and unknown location. First, there was shelter for the family. This could vary considerably. Usually, it was the house of the original failed owner who had lost the orchard in the Depression. One of the houses we lived in had only four very small rooms; another had four rooms and a kitchen. None had electricity, central heating, running water, or bathrooms. Heating and cooking would be from your own wood-burning stoves. Water came from a well or cistern and often had to be carried a long way to the house.

The next essential element was the ability to raise food for the family. Thus, a garden — or several gardens — were required. The family required enough space for tomatoes, green beans, lima beans, onions, carrots, beets, squash, cucumbers, lettuce, cabbage, corn, sweet potatoes, and the staple Irish potato. Of course, summer treats like cantaloupe and watermelon were snuck in if space permitted. It was the responsibility of the wife and kids not only to plant, tend and harvest these crops, but also to can, dry or preserve them in a form so that they could be used throughout the year. For staples like tomatoes, corn, and green beans, we used fifty or a hundred quart jars that had to be prepared, cold packed and cooked for four hours in the summer heat. Beans and onions could be dried and potatoes could be kept in a cool dark place all winter. Cabbage could be made into sauerkraut or buried in the ground in straw with their outer leaves to survive most of the winter.

In addition to a house and a garden, tenant farmers needed facilities to raise chickens for eggs and meat. Of course, the only dependable supply of meat for the family was the ability to raise hogs and cure the meat. If horses or mules were used on the orchard, this required that some hay must be raised, thus, there would be a barn. A cow or two could be kept for milk, cream and butter. In my father's longest and most stable job, raising cows became a larger effort with a share cropping arrangement with the investor. My mother also raised turkeys under a similar arrangement where half of the year's profit went to the investor.

This effort of self-sufficiency was a big and continuous job. The success and prosperity of the tenant family was determined by their ability to plan the effort along with the persistence and determination to carry through with nearly all of the work being done by the wife and kids. The husband's contribution was mostly done before and after his required ten-hour day. Occasionally he could make time during the work day for small annual jobs like plowing the family garden plot or planting the hay that feed the cow. Butchering day was the one day he took off of work to help with the family food. We had to plan for one of the coldest days of winter, when we could also get added help from friends and neighbors. The tenant would take one full day to kill the hogs and preserve the meat.

Of course, not all job locations provided all of these essentials adequately. Unfortunately, the true situation often became clear after the tenant had been hired and the family moved. As the facts became clear, many of these agreements lasted only one year. In my father's case this was true for two of his four locations. As the system was set up, it was virtually impossible to change in less than one year.

My father's last job was a major exception where he stayed for ten years. On this orchard, the second tenant's needs were not as well met and they changed every one or two years. This orchard also required one or two "day hands" that worked by the hour. The going rate was 12 1/2 cents an hour. The investor expected the tenant's family to fill these slots. My brother got his full $1.25 a day; I got $1.00 when I worked.

The summer grind consisted of spraying the trees and mowing the orchard. During the fall, winter apples were picked and packed and my father supervised as many as twenty or thirty workers. For the pickers, the going rate was 3 cents a bushel and for the workers in the packing shed it might be as high as $1.50 for a ten-hour day, with some variation among the jobs. I still got $1.00 a day but my father let me stay in school, so after school started I only worked on Saturday.

One of my mother's subsistence projects was to sell cream. She would milk two or three cows each morning and each evening, let the milk set overnight, skim off the cream each day and sell it at the end of the week. From all of this effort, after it was delivered to the creamery and tested for butterfat, she would get a ticket and a check for two to three dollars. This was used to pay for the family's grocery essentials, such as sugar, coffee, flour and soap. She would sometimes have eggs or butter to sell to the grocer. On a few occasions she would have to bring in my father from the car to pay the difference if she could not work out a "take-back" arrangement with the grocer and still keep what she thought she had to have.

As to the added "share cropping" that my mother and father did, without salary and beyond the ten hour day, I don't know any of the details concerning my father's arrangement with the cattle. Calves were sold and I suppose the profits were split with the investor in some manner. My mother raised the turkeys; the feed was charged at the feed store and paid off at the end of the season. For several years the remaining profit was split fifty-fifty between my father and the orchard owner.

In 1939 my mother made a stand and insisted that her share for the profit, $70, be used to buy the family's first radio: a four tube, battery powered, slant-front Philco. I now have this radio in my family room. After some renovation, it works very well.

In spite of this rather "lean" existence we were never destitute or even poverty stricken in the current sense. We were never hungry — that is without food. —though there were foods we didn't have as often as we would have liked. We had clothes, if sometimes made from feedbags, and a means to keep warm in winter.

My family, in fact, was far better off than many in the same circumstances at the time. This accomplishment was totally due to the good planning and hard work of my parents. I believe we were better off than some of our relatives that lived at a somewhat higher level with a bathroom and electric lights. It was not at all unusual for car loads of relatives to arrive, unannounced, on any Sunday summer day and all would be fed with an elaborate Pennsylvania-Dutch meal, prepared by the women from our garden, smokehouse, chicken house and cellar. I had heard my mother muse, as she washed up the final dishes in the evening, "We had twenty-three today." This was not a complaint; it was a statement of proud accomplishment.

We fit the cliché: "We were not poor, we just didn't have any money." That statement is easily and lightly said, but unless you have experienced that condition down to the bone, you don't understand. For me, the incident that I will always remember happened when I was nine. I attended a little four-room country school located a few hundred yards from a crossroads where there were two country stores. I had somehow come to learn that you could leave the school grounds and walk to one of the stores if you went to the principal for permission and explained how the purchase needed was necessary for your schoolwork. You could state your plan for getting there and getting back before the end of recess.

I had not had the need, or the nerve, to attempt this until I was in the fifth grade and then only under a special opportunity that arose out of charity. In the warmer months, the school had us all wash our hands before lunch. Without bathrooms, this was done by setting an old water cooler on the edge of the back porch. One selected student pushed the valve to dribble water on each set of hands as the line of students advanced. On the other side of the cooler another selected student held a jelly jar with holes punched in the lid containing soapy water, which was sprinkled on the hands along with the water. No towels were passed out, or available, so I guess we dried our hands on our clothes.

One day my teacher announced that they had run out of soap chips and if someone wished to bring in a cake of soap, it would be appreciated. Now to me, that was a valid reason to go to the store. I explained the need to my father and he gave me a nickel. I practiced my tale and chose the day to relate it to the principal. I got permission and was off on my quest during recess.

The special privilege of walking off the grounds, along the road and into a store, all by myself was something I had not done before. It was a real high. As I entered the first store I had to walk past the curved front of the candy case. It was located by the window to pick up the light and show off the large array of very colorful penny candy. I asked the price of soap to find that laundry soap was eight cents and face soap was five cents. There was no four-cent soap. I went to the other store to find the prices of soap were the same. I used my nickel to buy the five-cent soap, made my way back to school and presented the cake of soap to my teacher. She smiled and said, "Thank you, Glenvil, that is very thoughtful of you." Well, at the time, the pride of my generosity did not completely compensate for not having just one of those penny candies.

With time I came to realize this was the result of my poor planning. My mother would have found a penny for me if I had asked her, but the hurt of not having that penny at the time has always stuck in my memory. Of course, there have been many occasions since, where I was short considerably larger amounts of money but I will always remember that penny.

My Mother's "Luxuries"

In this family, spending $70 for a radio to please only my mother and myself, was indeed unusual since this was something that was not demanded or justified by its practical utility. There were other things that my father judged unnecessary — at least at first. In those last ten years mother had gotten a "modern" cook stove, a cream separator, an Aladdin lamp and a kerosene iron. Before that, she had gotten a washing machine. All of these came only after lengthy campaigns against my father's grumpy rejection. But we had to show how, even these "luxuries" were part of the day-to-day hard work. For example, the washing machine had been obtained under a plan that my sister would come once a week, in their Model T, and do her family wash with ours. A washing machine was a major step up from washing on a "washboard" which my mother had done up to that time.

Lottie DeHaven Whitacre

And for those who have only seen a washboard as a musical instrument in bad hillbilly bands, a washboard is a piece of corrugated metal set in a wooden frame with its legs extending at the bottom. This device is used by placing it against the inside of a washtub with its legs resting on the bottom. Now the washtub was a large tank, maybe three feet across, usually made of galvanized steel, capable of holding twenty or thirty gallons of water. When the water had been heated and soap added, the clothes were dumped in and each piece is lifted by hand and all parts of it rubbed on the corrugated surface of the washboard until the operator is satisfied that the dirt has been squeezed out. This had been a great step up from beating your clothes on a rock in the river, but it was very tiring and hard on the hands.

My mother eventually got an aluminum, square-tub washing machine with a gasoline engine to drive it. The water was heated in an iron pot in the yard with a wood fire built under it. Once warm, we carried the water in buckets and dumped it in the washer. Soap was added, the engine started (not always easily) and the first tub-full was agitated for several minutes. Then each piece of clothes was lifted by hand and fed into the wringer,

Not sure this is the exact model. Notice the gas engine on the bottom.

which was two rubber rollers powered by the engine, to squeeze out the soapy water from each piece and let it fall into a washtub of fresh water. After the clothes had soaked in the fresh water, the wringer mechanism was rotated around over the edge of the rinse tub and the pieces were fed again through the wringer to squeeze out the water and then dumped into a basket ready to be pinned up on a clothesline.

Even though this hand feeding of the clothes through the wringer was tedious (and dangerous, particularly to children, who could catch hands and even arms in the thing) the biggest job of wash day was heating and carrying the water, particularly since the well at the place we lived for those ten years was about a hundred yards away. The washer's soapy water would do two or maybe three loads if the clothes were separated by ascending color (lightest to darkest) and an inverse requirement for cleanliness (cleanest to dirtiest). The water in the rinse tub was left cold and was changed when it looked too soapy.

So for one run-through this was at least forty gallons of water to be pumped and carried in twenty two-gallon buckets a hundred yards from the well. Typically, at least two cycles were required for all of the farm-dirty clothes, requiring forty buckets full of water for the family's weekly wash.

The "modern" cook stove was a step up from the small cast iron model she had had since they were married in 1909. She moved the old stove to the summer kitchen for canning season. The new stove was quite attractive with its cream and pea-green porcelain covered sides. It had warming compartments above, a warm water tank on the end, and a temperature dial right on the oven door. A little eight-inch square firebox in its upper left-hand corner heated the stove. I suspect the engineers designed this to burn coal, but we didn't have any coal. We would have had to buy the coal. We only had wood and keeping a wood fire going in that small space all day and some of the night, to be restarted again before breakfast, was a talent that only my mother had.

Another "luxury" was the cream separator. It was the least expensive type, a gravity separator, which was just a vertical tank with little narrow windows down the side. My mother would dump the milk in the tank, let it stand for ten hours or so until the cream had risen to the top. Then by following the division between the cream and milk through the little window, the milk could be drained off and the cream saved to sell to buy the week's groceries. Of course, this procedure was repeated each morning and each evening every day of the week, all year.

The Aladdin lamp and the kerosene iron were really considered luxury items. The lamps commonly used in houses without electricity were oil wick lamps. The flame came from a wick an inch wide producing an orange flame of about the same width. The lower end of the wick was submerged in the bowl of kerosene, which fed up to the burner with a screw mechanism to adjust the height of the wick. The burner also held the base of a glass globe, which acted as a chimney, to supply the needed draft and when the wick

Aladdin lamp with its mantle created the equivalent of a 60-watt bulb.

was properly adjusted would sustain a steady flame. This produced about the equivalent of three candles. There is no way you could understand that amount of light today, unless you had seen a room lit by only one of these lamps. You could see someone across the table, but that was about as far as you could see. If you were an adult and allowed to carry a lamp, you could make your way up the steps to bed. Reading with the page held near the lamp was possible for the young, but not easy.

Coming away from centuries of even poorer lamps, the Aladdin lamp was a godsend. It had a circular wick about three inches in circumference and the burner held an inverted cone shaped mantel over the flame. This mantel was very delicate, made of knitted asbestos fibers, which once used, would fall apart if jiggled or touched. But it was this mantel that produced the magic of the lamp. When the hot blue flame from the wick heated the fibers of the mantel, they gave off a bright white light. As compared to the other lamps, this lamp was so bright that you never considered the atomic physics that changed the frequencies of the light emitted by the excited atoms of the mantel material; you just accepted this as magic and were grateful for the light. The intensity was about that of a 60-watt bulb. Yes, a godsend.

Now, as to the kerosene iron, this was a time before permanent press. Most clothing was cotton and a wife was expected to iron her husband's shirts, her dresses, the kids clothes and the sheets. This ironing was done by hand, one stroke at a time, with flat irons that were heated on top of the kitchen stove, summer and winter. Well first, how hot was the stove? The irons on the stove were always getting hotter and the one in use was getting cooler, so controlling the temperature of the iron in use was an art requiring frequent changes of irons. The kerosene iron was heated with a small burner inside that could be controlled by the flow of the kerosene. The burner was smaller but much like the Coleman camp stove, but while the camp stove burns gasoline, it was considered too dangerous to use gasoline in a device like this in the house. With kerosene, the burner had to be preheated with a large alcohol-soaked swab to get it started. This was a part of the task that even my mother would not attempt and that part was left to me. She loved that iron.

Penny Pinching

One might conclude, from what I have already said, that I thought of my father as a penny pincher. His money was all his own, held in secret and only doled out begrudgingly, if at all. Yes, that is true, but to have accomplished what he did in his life from his limited resources this was probably necessary. In the sixteen years he worked on orchards, he bought a new 1930 Model A Ford to take the family on its only trip, five hundred miles, to visit his brother Harry in Dayton Ohio. He bought a new 1936 V-8 Ford and then a 1938 Plymouth which served him for the rest of his life.

My father bought some three hundred acres of mountain land around his home place for almost nothing at tax sales. In those last ten years he was able to buy a forty-five-acre farm in the Shenandoah Valley with a barn, granary and a very old house. For this

Holmes Love Whitacre

273

he paid something over three thousand dollars. The house had been grand in its time but was in very poor condition by the time he bought it. In those final years, with his money, we were able to repair, rebuild and expand the house — even to add a bathroom.

My father kept both my brother and I in school, in a time and in an area where it was quite common for boys to be kept out to work during the apple harvest months. In fact, when it was time for my brother to attend high school, there was no free high school in that part of Virginia. He helped my brother buy a car so he could go to high school in West Virginia.

Then too, both my brother and I were able to go to college. My brother paid for it with a football scholarship, a job as a janitor to the girl's dormitory at his college, and his $1.25 for each ten-hour day of work on the orchard in summer. When this was not enough, my father would still give him money but this was done with his usual attitude. I remember witnessing one of these occasions when my brother needed money for lab fees and my father made him follow along the spray rig while it operated for a long time before he finally stopped and gave him the $25 from his wallet.

By 1941 when I started in high school, there was a free high school in Virginia. After graduation, I got help from the principal to get a working scholarship through a Baptist Church in Winchester, which paid my tuition. He also helped me get a summer government job that lasted the full four years. This government job started at the unbelievable salary or forty-seven cents an hour! As I advanced, my salary increased to ninety-six cents an hour in my final year. I was able to save this salary and it paid half of my room and board. When my father got a job driving a bus during the school year, he had his highest paying job ever of $100 dollars a month. Then he paid the second half of my room and board, about $300. This last sum was paid without my having to beg for it. But then, I did work full days on the farm and rebuilding the house through all those years in addition to my government job at night.

I was too young at the time to fully appreciate the challenges that surrounded my parents. I sometimes bristled at my father's tight control of the money but looking back I am amazed at the life he and my mother were able to make for our family.

Appendix

How Did He Make it to Adulthood? BINGO
The injuries and adventures of Glenvil Whitacre

B	I	N	G	O
Cut finger with a butcher knife losing control of second joint on his first finger, left hand.	Picked a ricocheted .22 caliber bullet out of his hair at a family Sunday gathering	Dropped a drawknife across his toes cutting through ligaments.	Showered with lime, arsenic and copper sulfate while walking behind the spray rig.	Bee stings from soldier bees of the orchard hives
Knocked a hornet's nest down on his bare back.	Jammed his finger in the apple sorting machinery.	Free Space	Landed on his head hanging from one knee from a tree.	Climbed inside a box on the back of a pick-up truck and was bounced off into he road
Fell through the kitchen ceiling while doing renovations - brought the ceiling with him.	Fell off the porch as a toddler and broke his forearm	Broke his front teeth on a downhill track his brother constructed	Passed out from sniffing gasoline from the gas tank	Didn't attend his fiancé's graduation because he was working on a Physics paper.
Nearly ripped his third finger off holding a generator while trying to start engine with foot.	Dropped a heavy Hot Shot battery on his foot causing a cut and infection	Temporarily blinded after a repurposed Model T gas tank blew up in his face.	Double Pneumonia before antibiotics	Wandering Philadelphia in the middle of the night with no place to stay.

Mrs. Whitacre Dies At DeHaven.

DeHaven, Feb. 20.—Mrs. Sarah Louise Whitacre, wife of Joshua Whitacre, died here at 2.30 o'clock Sunday. Mrs. Whitacre, who had been an unusually hale and hearty woman, contracted grip about Thanksgiving and from that developed typhoid fever which later ran into pneumonia. Five physicians and the most careful nursing, however, could not save her life. Deceased was the daughter of Thomas DeHaven, and the mother of nine children, all of whom are living. They are: Austin, Harry, Holmes, Tull, Edward and Lee and Miss Matilda, Miss Nita and Mrs. Mary Shade; and is also survived by her husband, Mr. Joshua Whitacre, and four sisters: Mrs. Anna Shade, Mrs. Dora DeHaven and Mrs. Mary Parlett, of this county, and Mrs. Jane Stotler, of Martinsburg, W. Va., and one brother, Mr. Charles DeHaven, of near Lew. Interment today in Chestnut Grove. Rev. Mark, her pastor, officiating, friends meeting at the house at 10.30 a. m. Deceased has been a member of the Methodist Church for twenty-three years.

Sara Louise DeHaven Whitacre Obit
Winchester Evening Star
January 20, 1906

Winchester Evening Star, June 15, 1907

YOUTH KILLED BY BIG WAGON

Young Edward Whitacre Is Run Over and Fatally Hurt in County.

THE VEHICLE OVERTURNED

He Was a Son of Mr. Joshua Whitacre, One of the Best Known Residents of Western Frederick County, and Has Many Friends.

(Special to The Star.)

Dehaven, Va., June 15.—One of the saddest deaths to occur in the western section of Frederick county occurred about 10 o'clock last night, when Edward Whitacre the 11-year-old son of Mr. Joshua Whitacre, was killed by an overturned wagon near his home.

The elder Mr. Whitacre had gone to Berkeley Springs on business, and his three sons, Austin, Holmes and Edward Whitacre, were pulling stumps in a field near the house with a heavy wagon drawn by four horses.

Wheel Passes Over Him.

The older brother was driving, and the two younger ones were attaching the chains to the stumps. Little Edward Whitacre fastened the chain he had been holding to a stump, and called to his brother to "go ahead." The horses made a sudden and unexpected surge and caused one of the rear wheels of the wagon to rise about three feet from the ground.

Without thinking, the little fellow ran to the wheel, caught the felloe to pull it back to the ground, when his feet slipped beneath the ponderous wheel just as the stump was torn loose from its stronghold.

The heavy wheel, with its extra force, came down on the lad's chest and face, knocking out one tooth and breaking his collar-bone.

Brothers To the Rescue.

The two brothers of young Whitacre hurriedly took him from under the wheel in an unconscious condition, and after shaking and rubbing him for some minutes he regained consciousness.

The boy expectorated a great deal of blood while he walked to the house—a distance of several hundred yards. Dr. N. R. Smith, of Gainesboro, was hurriedly sent for, and upon arriving set the boy's collar-bone.

It was then about 0.30 o'clock in the evening, and the child seemed to brighten up and appeared to be getting along nicely, continuing so until about 10 o'clock last night, when he asked his brother, Holmes Whitacre, to come and lie in bed with him, remarking at the time that he was about to die. The little patient expired in a few minutes—just seven hours from the time he was injured by the wagon overturning.

Father Sorrow-Stricken.

Mr. Whitacre was sent for, and was met only a few miles from his home. He was almost distracted when he came home and found his little boy dead.

Mr. Whitacre has had considerable trouble during the past few years, having lost his large barn, full of grain, by fire, and only several months ago his wife, who was one

(Continued on page 4.)

YOUTH KILLED BY WAGON.

of the most highly esteemed ladies of this county, passed away, and now the tragic death of his little son, who was a great favorite of his father, has caused Mr. Whitacre much sorrow, during which, however, he has the universal sympathy of a host of friends and acquaintances.

The funeral of the dead boy will be held at Chestnut Grove at 12 o'clock on Sunday, and interment will be made in the cemetery adjoining. Friends will meet at the house at 10 o'clock on Sunday morning.

278

Hollie Dehaven, aged 19 years, and the chief support of his widowed mother, lost his life last Thursday midnight by drowning in Back creek, 15 miles west of Winchester. Lee Clarke, who was with Dehaven, was rescued with a rope by Tina Braithwaite, a farmer living near the crossing, who heard the cries of the young men, who were clinging to a foot log. Dehaven lost his grip and was caught and carried down stream in a swift current. Their horse and buggy were rescued half a mile below the crossing. Clarke had gone to Harper's Ferry on Sarah Zane Fire Company's picnic. A cloudburst had converted all streams into torrents. The young men were warned to remain in Winchester over night, but young Dehaven's strong attachment to his mother, Mrs. Laura Dehaven, induced him to make an effort to reach home. The body was recovered the following day some distance down the stream.

Hollie DeHaven's Drowning
Shepherdstown Register.
Shepherdstown, VA [W. Va.]
August 09, 1906
Image provided by West Virginia
University

Clarissa Whitacre, Glen's oldest daughter with her niece Kate. Clarissa lives in Linthicum, Maryland.

Carla Whitacre Mayer with her son Luke Whitacre Mayer. Glen's youngest daughter and editor. Carla and her family live in Wheaton , Illinois.

Glen has two grandchildren who miss their "Gramps". Kate Whitacre Mayer and Luke Whitacre Mayer (photo about 2009)

Peter Mayer, Glen, Clarissa, Luke, Kate and Ethel during a beach vacation together

George, Virginia, and Velma are seated on the left. Glen is seated on the ground. Most are Velma's children, grand children and great grandchildren.

Family Memories Matter

After my parents died, I started helping people record their family stories. I conduct one-on-one or small group interviews. Sometimes I make an audio recording. Sometimes we work together to turn the interview into a little booklet with photos and documents.

No matter how young you may be, you have more history inside of you than you realize. If you are lucky enough to still have family elders, they have a world of stories you probably haven't heard. YOU can help save those stories for the next generation.

I've included below some good questions to ask yourself or your elders. Write. Talk into a digital recorder. Get your younger relations to video tape you with their phones. Whatever works for you.

As I was finishing my father's memoir, I was scheduled to interview a 92-year-old WWII veteran on St. Patrick's Day. He died a week before our interview. When I saw his obituary, I learned he was a long-time bartender near Chicago's historic Wrigley Field. He regularly served up-and-coming musicians who performed at the nearby Metro. I have no doubt he was a good storyteller and there will be a lot of people to tell his stories – but I still can't help but wonder how much better it would have been to preserve his stories in his own words.

Don't wait.

Interview and/or Writing Prompts

There are a vast number of books and online resources available to give you good questions. This is just intended to give you somewhere to start. Pick the questions that interest you.

1. What is the earliest home you remember? Was it an apartment, house, farm, or… ? Who lived with you?

2. What do remember about daily life as a child? Did you have chores? (favorite? Least favorite?)

3. In the summer, when you weren't in school, what was a day like for you? What was a day like during the school year?

4. How did you feel about school? Did you have a favorite teacher, coach or subject?

5. Did you have siblings? Tell us about your brothers and your sisters. What were your relationships like? Which sibling would you say you were closest to?

6. Did you have hobbies/activities/sports you liked to play as a kid?

7. Do you remember any particular road trip or vacation you took as a child?

8 What was your biggest challenge as a child?

9.What did you think you would do when you grow up?

10. Looking back, what do you think was wonderful about your childhood and what do you wish had been different?

11. Did you have a favorite relative or neighbor?

12. Did you family go to church or have any faith tradition? How did you feel about it?

13. How would you describe your mother (or father)? Did he/she work outside the home?

14. Did your mom or dad have favorite pastimes (cards, gardening, handiwork, bowling, etc.).

15. Do you have any particularly good or funny memory of your mom or your dad?

16. What did your parents teach you that helped you later in life?

17. What was your first "real" job? What was your worst job? Did you have a favorite job?

18. Did any family members serve in the military? What stories did you hear about their service?

19. Did you know your grandparents? Tell about a time you spent with them.

20. Did you ever hear any stories about your great grandparents? What did you hear?

21. Did your family strongly identify with traditions from another country? If so, describe them.

22. What are you most proud of in your life?

23. What would you like your great grandkids in the future to know about you?

Feel free to contact me if you have any questions.
I would love to hear your stories! Feel free to email me or tell me about your experience on my Facebook page.

For more information and tips on saving family stories check:
www.familymemoriesmatter.com

www.facebook.com/memoriesmatterinterviews

Acknowledgements

Thank you to my sister Clarissa Gwen Whitacre for being an anchor during my parents final years. She turned her life upside down to give our dad exactly the situation he wanted at the end of his life. Her strength, resourcefulness, and devotion was all any father could hope for.

Karen Kreiner Salser was an indispensable help getting this manuscript ready. She was a proofreader and, even more importantly, my encourager-and-chief through the publishing process. Thank you.

I am grateful to my husband Peter, and my children, Luke, and Kate, for allowing me time and space to finish this project. Yes, Kate, your mother can be really boring when she spends all day on her computer. Thanks for putting up with me.

This book would not have been possible without my father's careful preservation of photos and stories. I hope when he is finished being mad at me for editing his work, he will see this as a labor of love from a grateful daughter.

Glen and Ethel were married for 65 years.

CPSIA information can be obtained
at www.ICGtesting.com
Printed in the USA
BVHW041946010519
547101BV00013B/179/P